FRICTIONLESS

FRICTIONLESS

WHY THE FUTURE OF EVERYTHING WILL BE FAST,
FLUID & MADE JUST FOR YOU

CHRISTIANE LEMIEUX
WITH DUFF MCDONALD

HARPER
BUSINESS
An Imprint of HarperCollins*Publishers*

HarperCollins books may be purchased for educational,
business, or sales promotional use. For information, please email
the Special Markets Department at SPsales@harpercollins.com.

FIRST EDITION

Designed by Leah Carlson-Stanisic

Library of Congress Cataloging-in-Publication Data has been applied for.

ISBN 978-0-06-289367-3

20 21 22 23 24   LSC   10 9 8 7 6 5 4 3 2 1

CONTENTS

INTRODUCTION

When I was putting the finishing touches on this book in late 2019, the stock market was at record highs. It had also been recently overrun by unicorns. In start-up parlance, a unicorn is a privately held company that's valued at more than $1 billion. All in the span of a few months, several unicorns had tapped the public markets, including Lyft, Uber, Pinterest, Beyond Meat, and Zoom. While the spectacular collapse of the impending IPO of coworking juggernaut WeWork certainly put a chill in the market for new offerings as the year came to a close, that company's singular problems weren't going to permanently snuff out investor interest in healthy, fast-growing companies in the years ahead. Unicorns aren't going extinct. But from this point forth, it looks like they may actually have to build real businesses—with real profit margins. That's a good thing.

I launched my second startup, called The Inside, in the summer of 2018, and though my reason for doing so wasn't simply to try and create something worth a billion dollars, I, like many of my peers, watched in amazement as the founders of those unicorns saw their years of hard work ratified with meaningful public market valuations. It was, in a word, highly motivating.

But I was already motivated: the book you hold in your hands is a compilation of some of the most interesting conversations I've had in my life. At the very same time that I was trying to get my new company off the ground, I was interviewing dozens of start-up founders, academics, and experts of other varieties. In the process, I received a wide-ranging education in entrepreneurship—more than anyone deserves without having to pay for it.

One result of it all was that I found myself writing a different kind of book than I'd originally intended. I didn't start with a thesis and then confirm it via interviews. Rather, I let the conversations shape the thesis itself.

That's where *Frictionless* comes in. After I analyzed the content of more than six dozen lengthy interviews, I realized that while they were very different on the surface, they were all connected by a conceptual tissue called *frictionlessness* underneath. How so? Pretty much every single person that I spoke to was trying to reduce friction *somewhere*—and by that, I mean *everywhere*.

Some of them are reducing friction in their own business models in order to give themselves a competitive advantage. Others are offering a reduction in friction to their customers as a way to improve the customer experience and make the sale (and the one after that). And others are trying to figure out how to run companies—how they're organized, how to help them grow—so that we can all do a better job of staying out of our own way. Two final groups have set their sights on reducing friction on micro-and macro-levels. Those in the first are focused on helping every one of us live better lives, and those in the second are focused on trying to remove friction at a system-wide level, ironing out the bottlenecks in some of the most important realms where our lives intersect.

What are we doing at The Inside? We are digitizing the interior design process. By that I mean we are bringing a custom home-decorating experience, a process formerly reserved for people with means, to all consumers via technology. We saw potential to help customers bring their Pinterest boards to life. That is where The Inside comes in. We want to become the home brand of the Instagram generation. After all, why would you share a photo of a home that is lifted from page 27 of that big catalog you got in the mail when you could curate and design the space of your dreams and then share it with the world? Along with my cofounder, Britt Bunn, and the rest of our scrappy team, we're trying to reshape the entire industry, in large part by setting new standards for sustainable manufacturing and dragging a reluctant supply chain online. In the age of Amazon, custom furniture is one of the last of the consumer goods holdouts, the last industry to accept that consumers have moved online as well as the last to capitalize on all that the digital era has to offer in terms of design, manufacture, customer experience, delivery, and the rest of it.

I sold my first company, DwellStudio, to Wayfair in 2013 and spent two years as Wayfair's executive creative director before heading out on my own once again. Here's the crazy part: after spending nearly fifteen years building DwellStudio into a legiti-mate business, I could have written quite the playbook for some-one looking to do the same kind of thing. I am so relieved that I didn't, because the only thing it would be good for at this point would be starting a fire. There is no place now or in the future for that business model. In the span of just a single decade, it became defunct.

Why? Because *everything has changed.* Some of those changes have to do with technology (e.g., cloud computing), some with culture, and some with the Great Recession. No matter what the sources of change, the ways we think and do everything in business today—setting up a corporate structure, customer acquisition, communications (both internal and external), managing the supply chain—are all new.

I didn't want this book to be about me, though. I'm quite serious about that. Rather, I wanted it to be about the lessons themselves—what I'm learning each and every day about how to create a frictionless enterprise. To that end, I decided to base it not around my "story" but around a fascinating group of people much more interesting than me.

My coauthor, Duff McDonald, whom I have known for nearly thirty years, has written several bestselling business books. I've written two of my own, about design. But both of us agree that this one stands apart for the sheer number of great insights it has provided us. We hope you enjoy reading it as much as we enjoyed writing it.

And so, with the aim of a *frictionless* reading experience for you, dear reader, we're just going to get down to it without further ado.

—*Christiane Lemieux*

FRICTIONLESS

Chapter 1

WHAT DO WE MEAN BY FRICTIONLESS?

T he more I have thought about *frictionlessness* and talked about it with other people, the more I have realized that it's not just a choice that entrepreneurs *can* make. It's an *imperative*.

Of course, the forces of *frictionlessness* are not confined to the land of startups. Incumbent businesses must strive for *frictionlessness* as well to have any hope of survival. *All* businesses need to reduce *friction* if they're going to compete.

The same goes for each and every one of us, whether that's in how we, as individuals, react to the changing business landscape or how we strive to eliminate *friction* in the hopes of living more fruitful, healthy, and ultimately happy lives.

We're talking about an ontological change here, folks: we have entered a new era, and *frictionlessness* is the state of being that we're all aiming for, whether it's as individuals, as groups of people working together, or in the institutions in which we put our collective faith.

Every single one of the people in the pages that follow understands that a tectonic shift has taken place in the digital era, and it has to do with *time*.

Before the Internet came along, before it seeped into pretty much every aspect of our lives, we used to have to dedicate a set amount of time to all the various activities of any given day. This was particularly true for women, because of the domestic bondage that most mothers (including working mothers) found themselves in. Whether it was grocery shopping, bill paying, banking, or scheduling, there was no way around giving up a certain amount of time.

But the new citizen of the world is able to remove increasing amounts of the mundane from their daily existence using technology. It has changed the time equation in more ways than we can count. In doing so, it has given us a renewed understanding of the *value of time*—the most precious nonrenewable commodity that exists.

By eliminating *friction* from almost every task imaginable, we have been given back time, and we have reallocated it elsewhere. We are using that "found time" to do the things that really matter—like spending time with family or expanding our minds.

The main lesson of this book: If you hope to do business with anyone today, you best not be trying to claim some of that time back again. Because *you can't have it*. If there are too many pages on your website, if you ask customers for too much information, if the interface seems too jenky or the user experience unintuitive . . . *they are gone*.

So the move toward *frictionless experiences* isn't just a preference. It's a mandate. It's nothing short of a philosophical revolution that's been facilitated by that reallocation of time.

To those of us who were already adults by the time the Internet came along, many Internet-driven time-saving opportunities still seem a little novel—take, for example, the idea that it's possible to file an auto insurance claim without having to talk to a single person. But we're the last generation that's going to feel that way. For digital natives—that is, those born after the widespread adoption of digital technology—the idea of *frictionlessness* is part of their decision set. They don't know a world without it.

What do I mean by that? I mean that they will only *buy from companies* that give them the most optimal combination of best price, fastest service, and the least *friction*. If the experience has *friction* anywhere along the way, the digital human will drop off, abandon that cart, bounce from your home page.

They won't just bounce either. They will be *gone forever*—period, end of sentence. When there is friction involved, there is no second chance. That's partly because of the belief (whether or not it's true is another matter) that the Internet has brought us infinite choice. You are not the only option. And it's also because a frictionless experience is what we, as a society, have come to demand. We want seamless interactions, no matter what or where they are. If you can't deliver that, then you will eventually interact with no one.

Or you might not even get a chance at them in the first place. Consider what happened to The Inside in June 2019: for nearly six weeks, our traffic and conversion plummeted, and we couldn't understand why it was happening. It turned out that our inbound links from Google had broken, because our JavaScript was *newer than the one Google was indexing*. It was a pretty simple fix at the end of the day, but before we figured that out, it was as if . . . *we didn't exist*. If you are not on Google, you do not exist. If you don't provide a *frictionless* path to your digital storefront, you *do not exist*.

I'm not just talking about e-commerce, either. Those same digital natives will only *work for companies* that understand one of the most fundamental changes in the employer-employee relationship since the introduction of the forty-hour workweek. The trade-off used to be money for time—you pay them money, they give you their time. But those days are long gone. Today, you pay them money, and they give you their work. Their time is their own, and you best not come asking for it.

Time looks a lot different to people who don't know anything but Internet time. Those generations, more than their predecessors, have realized its true value, and they're not giving it away for free anymore. Those of us over forty have a unique vantage point about the tectonic transformation that's happened during our lives. It's why the whole idea of *self-care* struck so many of us as somewhat absurd—*Who talks like that? Who has* time *for that?* Well, it turns out that everybody does, because they're taking back their time from the people who have been taking it away from the rest of us our whole lives.

That's why at The Inside we are all about being *frictionless*, all the time. That includes how we work together, the customer experience, the growth (hopefully!) of the company, and the lives we all lead (yours, mine, everybody's). There's only one go-around on this ride, and nobody wants to get to the end and feel like they didn't make the right choices along the way.

Why should you decorate—or redecorate—your home? Because it's the place where you spend the most *time*. Because doing so makes you feel better. Human interaction with and within an incredible space is a remarkable thing. But many of us don't even bother with decorating because the experience is too overwhelming. It's laborious and time consuming. There are too many points of *friction*. When we say we are trying to *digitize decorating* at The Inside, what we really mean is that we're trying to strip the *friction* out of the decorating journey. That's it, in a nutshell: we are trying to remove *friction* and not ask for any more time than is on offer. We want to be part of the solution to the scarcity of time, not part of the problem.

We also strive for *frictionlessness* in the way we work: we moved our offices for The Inside in July 2018 into a shared space in New York's SoHo district. But even though the experience of moving in was quite *frictionless*, it turned out that our landlord hadn't gotten rid of all the friction: they played too much music, there weren't enough conference rooms, and we only had one window. My employees are vocal about what they want. It's no longer, "You're lucky to have a paycheck, now get to work!" but rather, "How much do *you*, my employer, make it easy for me to maintain the allocation of time that I demand if I am going to work for *you*?" And so we moved again in August 2019. Sure, part of the reason was that we were growing. We *could have* managed in the old space. The main reason that we moved was that there was too much *friction* in our workplace.

I can't stress enough, though, that the move toward *frictionlessness* isn't a temporary thing. While millennials didn't invent the time-saving technologies and systems that decimated the old way of doing so many things, they definitely internalized the profound implications of those changes before their elders did. The concept of being a slave to the clock, in which someone arguably *owns your time*, is over. Those shackles are being thrown off by the forces of *frictionlessness*, and only the foolish among us think they stand a chance of putting them back on. Practically everyone, from the CEO down to the janitor, has realized that *their time is as valuable to them as yours is to you.* So do what you want with your own time, but don't you dare waste mine.

By removing *friction* from the day to day of our lives, we can theoretically get time for the things we want. Harnessed properly, technology can provide a renovated architecture for our lives. *Friction* is what eats up time, whether it's in health care, education, leisure, or otherwise. Remove it, and we can get that time back. We may never get to the one-click life, but we can try.

Some people are already a step ahead of the rest of us. Every single person we have included in this book has figured out the interaction between *time* and *frictionlessness* before most of us did, and their stories hold lessons for us all:

- Don't you wish you could have that time you spent in line at the pharmacy back? Well, the folks at Capsule are ready to give it to you.
- Don't have time to put a full meal together for the entire family? Robert Wang's Instant Pot has solved that problem for millions already, with a big assist from Amazon.
- Want to live forever, but don't think you're going to? Gil Blander has been working toward that goal his whole life, and his company InsideTracker will help you do the same.
- Do you wish that you (or the woman in your life) could achieve orgasm more quickly? Well, Alexandra Fine and her team at Dame Products are helping women get there much faster than they otherwise might (or might not!) have done.

As you can see, we have covered all the important parts of a life well lived.

Having begun my second expedition into the wilds of version 2.0 of the American Dream—entrepreneurialism—I hope that this book can provide you with some help in navigating your own—or your children's—course into the future. Boldly. Because there's no other way to do it. Me? I feel like I stepped on an elevator and it's just continued going up.

One thing that I have found to be of immense value during this journey is my newfound focus on the sources and causes of change. Because it's those forces that open up new opportunity even as they demolish old ones. Some of the entrepreneurs you will read about in the pages ahead are using change to disrupt the business models of incumbent competitors. Others are using it to disrupt entire industries. A final category is using it to disrupt entire systems, whether it's health care, food, or the patriarchy. There are revolutionaries in the pages that follow.

It's also become quite clear to me that the future of innovation is being driven entirely by access to capital. I've had the good fortune of being able to raise venture capital money the second time around, and it's given The Inside the kind of leg up on the competition that most people would kill for. We're right smack in the middle of the institutionalization of entrepreneurship, a situation that did not exist when I started my first business. Neither did the landscape of disruption in which we all find ourselves—we knew about the Internet back in 2000, but few among us really knew what it all meant.

One refreshing change: Wall Street is not creating the real lasting wealth in our society anymore. Rather, it's coming from the companies that are mushrooming out of the venture capital peat—and the entrepreneurs who grow them. The ones that will succeed are the ones that know how to adjust to the new millennial reality—and that's a vastly different generational shift than those that have come before it. You either get it or you don't. You're either on the bus or you're not. You either provide a *frictionless* experience or . . . *you don't exist.*

Some of my younger readers may not know where the figure of speech "on the bus" comes from. It emerged during Ken Kesey's

LSD-fueled bus trips in the 1960s, and the dividing line was between those willing to surrender their ego to the power of hallucinogenic drugs (i.e., get on the bus) and those who weren't. Author Tom Wolfe captured the zeitgeist in his bestselling book *The Electric Kool-Aid Acid Test.* Fast-forward to 2018, and *New York Times* bestselling author Michael Pollan wrote *How to Change Your Mind,* a treatise on how the "new science" of psychedelics can teach us about consciousness and transcendence. The more things change . . .

But millennials really do seem to be living in different ways—and for different reasons—than their parents did. And the only way to succeed is to figure out both the *why* and the *how* behind those changes: So don't try to sell them a bus ticket; sell them a plane ticket to a three-day ayahuasca retreat in Peru instead.

Chapter 2

MY JOURNEY TOWARD FRICTIONLESSNESS

First Time Friction: DwellStudio

My coauthor Duff has a little dictum that he and his girlfriend Joey remind each other of as often as possible: "Always be wondering." It's their own version of "Stay Curious," a reminder to each other to keep their minds open. But they're not talking about having an "open mind" in the sense of being open to alternative points of view (although they try to do that too); rather, they're talking about wanting to always be learning, instead of closing their brains to new ideas.

I try to do that too. It's one of the reasons I decided to sell the company I spent thirteen years building to e-commerce giant Wayfair in 2013. Ask anyone who has built a thriving company from scratch, and they'll tell you that letting go is one of the hardest things you can do. When I signed the deal in July 2013, a flood of emotions surged through me. It felt like I was letting go of a huge part of my identity, leaving behind the beautiful world I had lived in for a decade and a half.

I was, however, very excited for the next chapter. Mainly because Wayfair, the dominant online brand in my world, was one

of those companies that doesn't come along that often. Along
with Amazon, they represented the future of retail. Wayfair had
dragged the worlds of furniture and design online, and I wanted
to join them. I knew I would learn a lot if I did.

I also knew it was time to sell. In the years since the financial
crisis, the retail world was suffering through an economic down-
turn of historic proportions, and, when you combined that with
the upheaval caused by the explosion of e-commerce, you had
to count yourself lucky if you'd even survived, let alone found a
willing buyer to bail you out of your particular predicament.

I didn't want to sell my company; I pretty much had to do so.
Even though DwellStudio was barely more than a decade old, it
was decidedly old school—mostly offline, capital intensive, and
built to succeed in a world where there were still offices, stores,
catalogs, and . . . sizable staffs. It was time to get out, but that
didn't make it an easy decision at all. I could have tried to raise
capital and attempted to continue on the trajectory I was on—
I've successfully raised two rounds of financing for The Inside—
but the problem with DwellStudio was that the business model
was no longer relevant. I couldn't raise money for something
that was showing slowing growth and declining long-term potential. DwellStudio had friction at almost every juncture in its
business model.

Let me back up and start at the beginning: I founded Dwell-
Studio not long after graduating from New York's Parsons
School of Design. I started pulling it together at my first job
post-graduation when I was a designer at Portico, a SoHo-based
furniture concept store. My lightbulb moment came when I was
working there. It gave me the opportunity to test some of my
designs at retail—I was obsessed with midcentury design long
before it became a thing—and they'd resonated immediately.

After that, I somehow summoned the courage to strike out on my own, to seize a white space and compete against established brands—and to have fun doing it.

I started the company in my apartment, by myself. I'm a classic entrepreneur in that it was almost an extension of my personality and passions. But also, like a classic entrepreneur—optimistic but delusional—I had no business going into business. I went to design school, and I didn't know a thing about business plans, Excel spreadsheets, or EBITDA (earnings before interest, taxes, depreciation, and amortization, for the newbies).

Was it fun to figure it all out? Most of the time—but not *all* of the time. To start with, I didn't have a mentor; I learned it all on the fly. When I started, I had no idea what a PO even was. So I had to learn fast: not long after we finally went to market (aka came out of beta) in March 2000, the orders started pouring in. Every single day, in one way or another, I was asking myself, "How do I do this?" With the help of my later partner Jennifer Chused, we learned everything on the job, from processing to accounting to shipping. Jenna taught me a lot about operations very quickly.

It took over my life too. You can't build a nationally recognized and respected brand without putting your nose to the grindstone and assembling a great team, and that's what we'd built. In 2013, DwellStudio products—highlighted by furniture, lighting, and bedding—were for sale in more than eight hundred specialty retail stores across the United States and Canada. Add to that a five-year partnership with Target, as well as catalogs, online, and licensing, and we ultimately became a worldwide wholesale operation.

The path we'd taken was a capital-intensive one—at the time I decided to sell to Wayfair, we had lots of inventory, significant office space, and a large staff. But we'd also reached a fork in the

road. If DwellStudio was going to make it to the next level—
from a boutique brand to one with real scale—we either had to
raise a ton of money, which would have been a first for me since
we had mostly bootstrapped Dwell from the get-go, or we had to
sell the company.

Like many other businesses grappling with the transition to
e-commerce, I also knew that we'd need to retool our operation
for a digital future, and the sooner we did that, the better our
chances of survival would be. But the thought of tearing down the
very thing I'd just spent thirteen years building in order to build
it back up again didn't seem like an enjoyable prospect to me.

I knew in my gut that our old business model was dead. We
could throw a bunch of cash at the thing to keep the doors open,
but unless and until the model had been overhauled, that approach would eventually stop working. Amazon was already
changing the margin profile of retail business, and our capital needs would one day bury us. DwellStudio needed to shed
all the dead weight: inventory, catalogs, and even people. That
would be a wrenching transition, and we might not even survive
it in the end. It would be safer to do so in the arms of a well-
capitalized acquirer, I concluded, than to try to do it on our own.
And so I decided to sell.

Wayfair didn't offer us the most attractive deal, financially
speaking. But it was the best from a strategic standpoint—for the
company, the employees, and me. While still a private company,
Wayfair had already run away from the pack when it came to
selling home furnishings online; the company's $600 million in
2012 revenues left established offline brands like Crate&Barrel,
Williams Sonoma, and Restoration Hardware in its dust.

Wayfair's closest online competitor, One Kings Lane, had
built a business on the flash sales model of e-commerce giants
like Vente-Privee and Gilt, and had helped prove that people

were willing to buy home furnishings online. But One Kings Lane lacked Wayfair's sophisticated back end, which seemed of utmost importance to me. (I was right: One Kings Lane was sold to Bed Bath & Beyond for a mere $12 million three years later, whereas Wayfair's market capitalization at the time of this writing was $12 *billion*.)

The way I saw it, by selling to Wayfair, I was putting both the brand and my employees in the best hands and putting myself in a position to learn all I could from one of the most visionary people in e-commerce, Wayfair CEO Niraj Shah. If you're trying to *always be wondering*, it doesn't hurt if you're hanging around a focused and disciplined idea-generating machine like Niraj.

Had I managed to create a unicorn—a private company with a valuation of $1 billion or more? Alas, not even close. But I was selling to one, and part of the purchase price came in the form of pre-IPO stock. I'd been chasing my own unicorn for more than a decade, and it didn't seem like such a bad consolation prize to end up riding somebody else's.

A Frictionless Mind: Wayfair

I sat on Wayfair's executive team for two and a half years, from August 2013 to December 2015. It was an exciting time; I was there when the company went public. While I'd like to think they learned a little something from me, the fact of the matter is that I received an elite education in e-commerce from one of the most forward-thinking companies in the space.

What's the lesson here? I'd made somewhat of a name for myself in home furnishings. I'd sold my company to an e-commerce giant. I'd already signed a contract with Clarkson Potter to write *The Finer Things*, my second book, which garnered rave reviews and established me as a bestselling author on design. But I also knew that I didn't know what I didn't know. One of the reasons I stayed at Wayfair was financial: I needed my options to vest. But the other reason I stayed there was because I knew I wasn't ready to take my next step, and I could hardly ask for a better way station than a place that wasn't just taking the next step but blazing the trail itself.

I know it sounds a little trite to write in a business book that it's important to find good mentors. But so be it: it's one of the most important pieces of advice I can offer any would-be entrepreneur. No matter what stage of your life you're at, no matter how much you love or hate your current boss or the people you work with, there will always be something you can learn from them. I got lucky. Niraj was the perfect mentor for me at the perfect time.

But it wasn't just him. Wayfair's entire team is so good that it took them less than a month to onboard our website onto theirs and go live—this after the president of one of their competitors had told me that it would take two years for them to do the same. That would have been a miss of colossal proportions, and it reinforced my conclusion that Wayfair was going to win in home furnishings online. I was right: Wayfair's revenues took off, jumping from $600 million in 2012 to $915 million in 2013 to $1.3 billion in 2014.

By Niraj's calculations, there were 275 million households that had the income to buy products on Wayfair. The market was about $200 billion in size, and only about 20 percent of it had moved online. That's a $160 billion gap, and no one was touching it. No one else saw what they did at the time. No one.

Keep in mind, in 2013, home furnishings was one of the few remaining consumer categories that hadn't been completely disrupted by the shift to e-commerce. At the time, Wayfair still had to beg some people to sell them product, because the furniture industry was still laboring under the illusion that nobody was going to buy a sofa online. Just like Amazon, Wayfair was chasing the transactional, selling lots of everything, as easily and frictionlessly as possible. But their process was dependent on a search algorithm, and, like all search algorithms, it generally surfaced product options based on reviews, past sales, and time spent on the site. In this equation, the consumer loses; such an algorithm can be great at selling product but much less so at inspiration and giving people the tools to create something authentic and personal. And when it came to creating their home, I felt that consumers really wanted more: more inspiration, more quality, and—most important—more design.

But I still had a lot to learn: when I suggested that we needed to re-photograph every SKU on the Wayfair site to upgrade our digital assets, they scoffed at the idea, asking me if I knew how much it would cost to re-photograph 13 or 14 million products. They were right. While I'd been around the block in the design world by that point, I'd never been involved with an operation of that size, something commonly referred to today as "venture scale."

I'd always known that I wouldn't stay at Wayfair forever. It wasn't that I didn't think they had a bright future—they did, and they still do. And while they'd purchased DwellStudio in order to beef up their in-house visual design capabilities, it was clear to all involved that Wayfair was never going to stray too far from its engineering roots. Design will always be a secondary consideration for them, and never the primary one. I'm a designer at heart. I'm also an entrepreneur, and any entrepreneur can tell you that once you've been your own boss, it's never going to be easy to report to someone other than yourself.

Deep down, I knew that the first company I'd built was already a dinosaur by the time I sold it. But instead of wallowing in self-pity over the fact that I'd had to relinquish control of my brand, I used my time at Wayfair to understand the reasons why. Because I knew it wasn't just about me, or about DwellStudio. The same kind of tough choices were being forced on pretty much everybody, successful brand or not. My tenure at Wayfair was a time to reflect, to wonder, and to learn from those around me. I was going to figure out what I could do, what I couldn't do, and what I might be able to do. I sought to release my mind from the shackles of habit and experience and set it loose in the realm of future opportunity.

The question every seasoned entrepreneur wants an answer to was always there, in the back of my mind: Was there a way I could start a new business without all the pain points I'd run into the last time around? I made a list of all the horrible points of friction that I'd run into with DwellStudio's business model that had stopped me from scaling into infinity. Could I address (or even eliminate) all of them and just do the one thing that I love—design—and help make every home a little more beautiful along the way?

My Points of Friction

Point of Friction #1: Inventory. The perils of excess inventory are so well documented. In 2013, the only way to squeeze enough margin out of an inventory-based home furnishings business was to have everything made largely in China. The problem with that is that Chinese factories generally require huge minimum orders. If you're going to make the quantities necessary, you have to place big bets that your designs will resonate with consumers. The winners are great but the losers are really hard to endure. And unless you have incredibly talented inventory planners, you will find yourself with not enough winners (leaving money on the table) and too many losers (which you need to be able to absorb). You also need to be able to place product (i.e., the losers) with discounters to liquidate your excess inventory, which inevitably degrades the brand. It's a very stressful cycle.

Point of Friction #2: Production Time. An inventory-based model also leaves you unable to react to the market in any meaningful way. Traditional product development cycles are typically eighteen months, which, in today's accelerated consumer landscape leaves you unable to capture trends, especially in competition with the new phenomenon of single-SKU social media brands—think toothbrush companies like Goby or Quip—designed for quick trend drops.

In recent years, we have seen the hyperacceleration of trend. Companies such as Choosy use artificial intelligence and algorithms to identify the top trends across a myriad of platforms (think Instagram and Pinterest) and then manufacture them within weeks. Choosy asserts that its fashions are "guaranteed to be liked"—they are *generated from* social media and, likewise, *generated to* optimize social media. The tail now wags the dog. The days of protracted design and production cycles are over. This is faster than fast fashion, a tectonic shift made possible due to a lack of infrastructure (stores, catalogs, and advertising) and as a result of technology (a digital and direct-to-consumer model).

Point of Friction #3: Wholesale. The cost structure around maintaining a wholesale business is difficult. You need to go to trade shows four times a year or more. You need a staff to take care of it, as well as outside sales reps to visit stores and keep the fires stoked for the new product coming in. We sold to 810 stores across the United States. Add all that up, and you're talking about big money. That's why furniture gets marked up 3.5 times and then discounted according to demand. To operate a wholesale business, you need a ton of margin, and the consumer now knows that they are paying for it. Our five-year stint with Target was so much easier—one customer, two to three collections a year, a seamless and profitable relationship. We made ten times the amount from selling through Target than from the rest of our wholesale business.

Point of Friction #4: Photography. One of the most significant costs in home furnishings or fashion is your photography costs. They're astronomical. And the bigger you get, the crazier these costs become—at DwellStudio, it was up to 20 percent of our cost, and I can only imagine what it runs at a photo-centric retailer like Restoration Hardware. Once you get to scale, spending can become a runaway train.

Point of Friction #5: Shipping. Thanks to Amazon, the consumer now expects free and fast shipping, putting pressure on everyone's margins in the process. But there's nothing you can do about it—it's table stakes in e-commerce. If you try to add shipping costs into the checkout process, you invariably create friction and ultimately cause a loss of sales.

Point of Friction #6: Exclusivity. If you are not producing your own product and you have to stock inventory, you are going to be carrying the same assortment as your closest competitors. All the major e-commerce retailers buy from the same suppliers, which results in a race to the bottom.

Frictionless Furniture: The Inside

As most readers know full well, in the decade and a half since I'd founded DwellStudio, *everything* had changed. The spread of the Internet had thrown the world of business—rather, the *entire world*—into an industrial revolution-sized metamorphosis, a massive shift and reconfiguration of how we go about almost every aspect of our lives. Anthropologists will look back at this time as one of just a handful of seminal moments in the history of mankind, when everything turned on a dime, and nothing was ever the same again.

It was a challenging time for any CEO, as technology was in the process of demolishing most of the ways we'd done business to that point. At the same time, however, ambitious entrepreneurs were using technology to rebuild those same businesses from the ground up. There was a revolution going on, and I wanted in. I wanted to be one of those people—the courageous types who created the future instead of simply letting it happen to them. They are *the wonderers*—that is, the people who invent new categories instead of simply fighting for the dwindling scraps left in the old ones. In my world, I'm thinking of people like Rent the Runway's Jennifer Hyman and Jenny Fleiss, Airbnb's Joe Gebbia and Brian Chesky, or, dare I say it, Uber's Travis Kalanick.

But I also knew that if I wanted to do that, I needed to learn how to think like a disruptor. I didn't stay at Wayfair too long—just two-and-a-half years—but it was enough time to prepare myself for reinvention. I won't say I went through an identity crisis, because that wasn't the case. It's more like I went through an identity shift. Before Wayfair, I'd seen myself as a designer—of textiles, interiors, and fashion—but I suddenly realized that the digital revolution had given me an amazing opportunity.

Problem-solving is a characteristic of most entrepreneurs, yet to that point, the problems I'd been trying to solve were mainly problems of design. But I realized I could remold myself into a different kind of problem solver. I could take a run at fixing a broken business model. I was going to try and break ground not just in the realm of design, but in *every single part* of the business—design, manufacturing, sustainability, fulfillment, employment, company culture, and otherwise.

It's an enervating challenge—similar, I would guess, to that facing diagnostic physicians: *Which symptom or problem do you attack first for the greatest possible outcome?* But I felt that doing so would be far more fascinating than simply sticking to the designing I'd been trained to do.

I left Wayfair in December 2015. I left some money on the table, because not all of the stock they had paid me had vested, but the time had come for me to get back out there on my own. To recharge, I took a short vacation (if you're chasing unicorns, there are no extended vacations), spent another five weeks thinking about my plan, and then picked up the phone and started making calls.

The first ones were to a few key suppliers from my Dwell-Studio days. "I'm going to change the way people buy custom furniture," I told them. "Do you want to do it with me?" I'd worked with a number of them for almost fifteen years, so a few were willing to take a flier with me. Provided that I could figure out what I wanted to do. And if I could raise the money I'd need to do it.

The plan: I decided to found a new company—we later landed on the name The Inside—that would be a premier seller of well-designed home goods to digital-first customers, including millennials. On the surface, that might sound a lot like Dwell-Studio, which was also a premier seller of well-designed goods, but to a small, design-savvy cohort of midcentury enthusiasts with significant disposable income. But millennials are not like those of us who came before them. At the same time that the Internet has blown up all the business models, it has blown up all the career models—actually, the *life* models—as well.

The careers of tomorrow aren't going to look anything like the careers of yesteryear. And pretty much everybody knows it: only 19 percent of companies recently surveyed by Deloitte report that they still have a traditional career model.[1] Whereas the typical career in generations past might have included jobs at four or five companies, today's college graduates will work for that many in their first ten years post-graduation.[2] And the World Economic Forum estimates that 65 percent of children today will end up in careers that don't even exist yet.[3]

Is the whole idea of a four-year college obsolete? That question deserves its own book, but I do know this: there is nothing about the way they taught college in the 1980s and 1990s that could have prepared us to steer the raft of one's career in the swirling whitewater that is business and life today.

So this should not surprise: Syracuse professor Robert Thompson, an expert in popular culture, says that the idea of creating a startup "is taking up a larger and larger role in our aspirational lives."[4] Indeed, 70 percent of millennials want to eventually launch their own companies.[5] A 2017 study reported that self-employment is likely to triple to 42 million workers by 2020, with 42 percent of them millennials.[6] That aligns quite nicely with other studies, which have also shown that the key to happiness at work isn't money—it's autonomy.[7]

Or, put another way, it's *flexibility*. The millennial citizen wants—nay, demands—flexibility in all aspects of their lives: as employees, as customers, as dating partners. Millennials haven't just eschewed the idea of permanent fixtures; they have, by virtue and necessity both, embraced impermanence in ways that make those of us who came before them seem like that kid in kindergarten who wouldn't share. They'll share (or rent) just about anything—cab rides, apartments, even furniture. Self-driving cars might be the ultimate form of sharing, where they're prepared to cede (i.e., share) control of their vehicular fate not to another person but to a machine. As CEO of The Inside, I can barely contain myself when I think about self-driving trucking. Talk about cutting costs out of your supply chain!

The term "rent versus own" used to refer to one thing—the

place you live. These days, it might refer to *anything*, whether it's clothes, cars, or music. Here, and elsewhere, the purchase decision has been turned inside out. Permanence ain't what it used to be. Generation X has given way to Generation Flex.

What does that all mean for The Inside? It means that we are designing for a much more itinerant customer, one that might not *ever* feel in a position to buy a $5,000 sofa or a $3,000 bed. It also has implications for how we run the business itself: if The Inside is going to survive, the jobs and opportunities we offer our employees are going to have to track well with the new paradigm. While I'm not offering people the chance to be self-employed, I better be damn sure to provide the other things this generation demands: autonomy, flexibility, and respect.

At Wayfair one day, I was stunned to turn a corner in the office and find a couple of engineers sleeping on sofas, right smack in the middle of the day. Today's key employee no longer conforms to the office culture anymore; the office culture conforms to them. Our head of engineering lives in Medellín, Colombia, because he is talented and flexible and shares our vision. That ethos is driving migration to once-secondary US cities—a dollar stretches a lot further in Austin, Texas; Athens, Georgia; or the *other* Portland (Maine), than it does in San Francisco or New York. And when it comes to hiring locally, startups like The Inside must compete for talent with the likes of Facebook and Google. It's difficult to contend with their financial packages.

The connected world really does allow you to extend your company to where the talent is, instead of trying to lure everyone to you. You want another example? I don't think it would be possible to hire a US-based 3-D modeling team like the one I have in Eastern Europe, a region, formerly under Soviet influence, that is still reaping benefits of a rigorous mathematics curriculum to this day.

What's the most important thing I can tell you about the differences between building DwellStudio and The Inside? That nothing is the same—nothing whatsoever. And I'm not just talking about home furnishings—I am talking about everything:

1. All the things you need to do to get started.
2. The very nature of competition.
3. Your relationship with your customers—each and every one of them.
4. The new world of marketing.
5. The new world of employment.
6. The social responsibility of a modern company.

All that said, I want to deliver some good news: *it's never been easier to start a new business.*

I used to have to employ a staff of twenty-five to do what I do now with a team of five people. The rest is outsourced. Consider the following: on a hot summer day in July 2018, during the final crucial days of a nine-week venture capital fundraising effort, The Inside moved from our first office in Tribeca to a co-working space in SoHo without ceasing operations in any way. It took us just one day. Imagine what that would have taken in the year 2005—finding a place, negotiating a lease, three months deposit, setting up your utilities, moving over your IT infrastructure. Our operating expenditures are as light as a feather—we pay rent, but no utilities, no power bills, no nothing. Just one flat fee. (As I've already explained, we moved again a year later, but the point remains the same: we needed less friction, and we got it. Eventually, we needed even less than that, and we got it again.)

We don't have any technological hardware beyond our laptops and cell phones—we don't have servers or the IT staff that used to take care of them. Everything is in the cloud—from our e-commerce platform to our customer service chatbots. Some of the things that cost an arm and a leg just a decade or so ago, such as enterprise software and website development, have become some of the most inexpensive parts of the business. We created a sophisticated working website on the Shopify platform in less than two months and then migrated to our own build just as quickly.

But here's the bad news: *it's never been harder to keep a new business on track.*

That holds true for almost all businesses, but let me talk about my own particular niche in retail. There used to be a time when retailers could reasonably consider themselves masters of their own fate. These days, that's only partly true. Because today, we are all beholden to the algorithm. Rather, *all of* the algorithms— the ones behind Google search; the feeds of Facebook, Insta- gram, and Twitter; and every single decision Amazon makes about its platform.

More than a few businesses have seen their revenues evapo- rate overnight because someone at Google or Facebook tweaked an algorithm. Poof! You're gone. In the year through April 2019, Apple shut down eleven of the top seventeen screen-time and parental-control apps—not for the good of society but for the bottom line.[8]

In short, the nature of competition has been irrevocably changed. Size used to matter, at least in retail. So you wanted to start a new company and compete with Walmart? Good luck with that. These days, it's all about who optimizes their marketing and customer acquisition costs most effectively, and that's a realm where size only matters so much. *Frictionless* is now king.

Because of that, some of the smartest entrepreneurs aren't creating new businesses out of whole cloth but simply disrupting the old ones, finding categories with customer *friction*, bringing them online to take out the woes, and then marketing fiercely to grab market share from incumbents.

These are people who aren't just asking the big questions; they're answering them too.

What does it mean to live in this new world?

How can you optimize for the New American Dream?

Nobody's got all the answers, but I've crammed as many as I can into the pages that follow.

Farewell to Friction

At The Inside we like to say that our goal is to *digitize decorating*. But what we really mean by that is that we're eliminating friction from both the front and back ends of our business. The back end is our business model. The front end is the consumer-facing storefront.

My first idea was to sell B2B, or wholesale, but I ditched that after realizing that most of the efficiencies get lost if you go wholesale. I wanted to squeeze *all of the margin* out of the supply chain. If I wanted to do that, I had to sell straight to consumers. So we don't have wholesale accounts, and we don't have outside salespeople. We don't do trade shows.

On the business model side, we eliminated friction everywhere we could:

Design: We design everything "virtually." My design team is dispersed, and the product design process takes place in the cloud—we don't make physical product until we've already sold it.

Inventory: We have thousands of items on our website, and there is almost no cost to us until the consumer hits "Buy." We have zero inventory. We only manufacture the furniture after it is purchased. It's better for the customer and much better for the environment.

Manufacturing: Manufacturing exclusive designs on demand solves the inventory and selection challenge at the same time. When you manufacture on demand, you don't have an inventory problem, because you don't have any inventory at all. But that doesn't mean we can't offer a wide selection. It's *because* we manufacture on demand, with a complex but nimble supply chain, that we can carry a wide and curated selection that isn't narrowed by the need to manage an inventory position. Our selection challenge isn't that we don't have enough; it's that we have to make sure we don't offer so much as to cause decision paralysis. We address that challenge by using machine learning to understand how our customers choose what they buy and when they buy it.

Fixed Costs: We don't have landlines, a network, or any other IT infrastructure. Visit our office and you'll have trouble finding a sheaf of paper that's being wasted. Don't bother looking for one in the printer, either, because we don't have one.

Logistics: Everything that can drop-ships: we hold no inventory, and orders are transmitted directly to the manufacturer, who ships the goods directly to our customers.

What does that all mean for the consumer-facing storefront?

When I say that we squeezed margin out of the supply chain, what I mean is that we eliminated almost all of the friction of buying a piece of custom furniture, save for the manufacture and the delivery. And in the custom-furniture business, there were a lot more opportunities to do so than you might think.

Let me take you through the way it used to work:

- You wanted a custom sofa.
- You hired an interior designer.
- You accompanied them somewhere like the Decoration & Design Building in New York, showcase to thousands of manufacturers and dozens of individual showrooms.

- You went through twenty-five or so showrooms and hopefully found a sofa and a fabric that you loved.
- You tried to order the fabric—the jargon is COM, for customer's own material—and you crossed your fingers it was in stock. If it wasn't, you were talking about a fourteen-week wait.

Let me stop there for a second. I cannot tell you how many sales we left on the table at DwellStudio because our leather manufacturer was out of stock. That one supplier alone was probably responsible for $100,000 of lost sales.

- The fabric manufacturer sent the fabric COM to the workroom that made the sofa, they upholstered it, then your designer figured out how to get it to you, typically via white-glove delivery. The whole process took at least fourteen weeks. If you were lucky.

So . . . that's: designer, showroom, FedEx of fabric, manufacture, FedEx or white-glove to you. In that value chain, no one is taking less than a 50 percent margin, and FedEx might even touch the product two to three times. Not only that, if your fabric is $125 a yard, you need to add the interior designer's own markup as well. That's how a $1,500 sofa ends up costing $5,000.

Here's how it works at The Inside:

We function as your designer. We make the fabric and the furniture at the same place, on demand, and ship it just once, by FedEx, to you. There is no waste on the inventory front. We require the minimal level of shipping possible, resulting in a dramatic reduction of the carbon footprint.

Add all that together, and we're able to offer our customers something many of them have never had access to before: a service and product that has historically only been available to people who hire fancy high-end decorators. We stripped out everybody else's markups, and we have passed those savings on directly to our customers. And we don't just save our customers *money* in the process, we also save them *time*, both on the front end (choosing and designing) and the back (shipping).

As you can see, I'm obsessed with friction and bottlenecks, and with trying not to be one myself. That means building the right team, the single most important thing an entrepreneur must do. Britt likes to point to an observation by legendary venture capitalist Vinod Khosla: "The team you build is ultimately the company you build." I could not agree more. Hiring really good people in key roles right from the beginning will, in most cases, be the difference between early success and failure.

While the particular positions will vary depending on industry, these are the ones that were crucial to getting The Inside off the ground:

A Talented Cofounder: In this day and age, it doesn't hurt to have a great cofounder. Two minds will always be better than just one. And if your cofounder has a complementary skill set to your own, that can be game-changing. Mine is Britt Bunn, who runs the operation. A graduate of Stanford Business School and veteran of Bain & Company and One Kings Lane, Britt is a force multiplier and the partner I wish I had on my last business too.

Creative Director: When you're in the design business, having a talented creative director is obviously an imperative. At The Inside, we have Danielle Walish. I've worked with Danielle for so long that all I need to do is look at her and we've already had the conversation.

Should you hire MBAs? That's an interesting question for the team that co-authored the book. Duff has written critically about both management consulting firms and MBA programs in his books *The Firm: The Story of McKinsey and its Secret Influence on American Business* and *The Golden Passport: Harvard Business School, the Limits of Capitalism, and the Moral Failure of the MBA Elite*. (As you can see, he does not mince words.) *I agree with Duff* that a lot of great minds are going to waste chasing credentials and bonuses in the career Venn diagram that is Consulting/MBAs/Finance. But *Duff agrees with me* that both MBA programs (the good ones, that is) and management consulting firms do produce a kind of structured critical thinking that can be crucial for startups, where you need as many people as possible who are nimble at seeing problems (current and future) and developing solutions to challenges that few, if any, experienced managers have even seen before. E-commerce 3.0 is all about solving problems that we're all seeing for the first time, and the more people you have with the ability to do that systematically, the better off you will be.

Our roster keeps growing, too, with the additions of Jessica Jakobsson in product development and Lindsey Schmidt in public relations. By the time this book is published, we should have about twenty carefully selected colleagues. Nothing gets in the way of growth like intra-company friction, so we are constantly tweaking our mix.

Of course, we've already made a few missteps, and we're barely getting started. Our first office was a cool old loft on Walker Street in Tribeca. When we signed the lease, I was still stuck in the idea that you needed a physical presence in the design business, a showroom for customers to visit. That was a $15,000 renovation and $9,000-a-month mistake. While people still want to see swatches when they're buying furniture, most of them don't really want to come visit you. Even the showroom has gone digital. Britt put it best when she told me that the showroom was a sunk cost. We had to see if it was going to work out or not, whether having one would add to customer conversion. Well, it turns out that it doesn't. We still send out swatches—there's an 18 percent bump in conversion from doing so—but other than that, we could do this from anywhere, just us, our cell phones, and our computers. Everything else is in the cloud. We might do a pop-up showroom or a store down the road, but at the moment, we are as digital as they come.

The Frictionless Future

Running a startup is hard, but the new reality has made it even harder. There are days when I fantasize that I hadn't done it at all, but instead gone to work for *Architectural Digest*, writing a monthly column on design. It would be easier than starting a new business, that's for sure. And I'm pretty sure it would have made me happy. It's not like the statistics are in our favor either: one quarter of startups don't survive their first year, more than half don't make it to year five, and more than 80 percent don't survive a decade.[9] Those are daunting odds. But they're not low enough to give up on a dream. A 2013 survey, conducted globally, found that successful entrepreneurs are among the happiest people on earth.[10]

But let's get back to our customers for a moment, and the elephant in this generation's room: All. That. Debt.

The *New York Times* offered up some sobering statistics in August 2018:[11] home ownership among Americans in their twenties and thirties is near a three-decade low. Just 35 percent of households headed by someone younger than thirty-five owned a home in 2017, a precipitous decline from 42 percent in 2003. Today, they're much more likely to be living with their parents.

Why? Here's one reason: the average student now graduates with $22,000 in debt.[12] And they're running into problems paying it back: among graduates of for-profit colleges, 44 percent of borrowers were facing some kind of loan distress five years into repayment, with 25 percent in default.[13]

Somewhere along the way, the American Dream of a college education leading to secure and satisfying employment and careers turned into a Shakespearean Shylock nightmare: At $1.4 trillion, the country's student loan bill recently eclipsed credit cards to become the largest source of personal debt outside mortgages. It's more than *five times* the amount it was in 2003. This is just crazy. An entire generation is being enslaved into debt by a system that no longer guarantees anything in return.

Again, the current societal metamorphosis has *everything*: we're not simply watching dramatic changes in the nature of business but in everything else as well: careers, debt, homeownership, and more. And as a retailer, every single one of those issues is central for my industry. We sell *furniture*, after all—to millennials, who are going to experience a whole new kind of career churn and move countless times in their lifetimes. That transient nature has everything to do with my business. And while at first blush, it might seem like a disaster—if nobody's buying homes, who is buying furniture?—upon closer inspection, there's a niche there just waiting to be exploited. In the past, people didn't buy furniture at a regular cadence; first came the real estate, then came the big-ticket investments in a sofa, beds, tables, and chairs. That's how the price of a sofa has stayed so high for so long.

But what happens if there's no "big-ticket" purchasing moment? What if the life of a millennial is instead going to be filled with a series of smaller, more affordable purchases? The average price of a sofa seems destined to come down. And maybe, just maybe, the number of less expensive sofas sold is going to head in the other direction. That's where we come back to good design, which is what you will find at The Inside. It's all circular.

I can try to predict the future along with everyone else, but the fact of the matter is that as the world keeps changing around us, most people don't quite know what's happening *today* anymore, let alone *tomorrow*. I can't see the future, but I do know what it feels like to be an old-school (i.e., pre-Internet) entrepreneur who's in the midst of transforming herself into a new-school one. There's a lot of *friction* when you try to transform yourself; the best among us find a way to eliminate it, to bring *frictionless* change to the way we see the world and engage with it.

In that spirit, I hope that *Frictionless* can serve as a guidebook not just for the intrepid would-be entrepreneurs out there, but for everyone else as well. How can you prepare your children for a world that you can barely keep up with yourself? For starters, you can *always be wondering*. While I hope my own experience can serve as an interesting example in its own right, I think that the combined experience and insight of anyone who is in the trenches *today* is where the real magic lies. To that end, the rest of this book is really about *People Who Are Far More Successful Than Me*.

Chapter 3

THE FRICTIONLESS ELEPHANTS
Amazon, Apple, Facebook, and Google

I'm not here to tell you that Amazon, Apple, Facebook, and Google are four of the most important companies in history. You already know that, and their market valuations attest to it quite clearly.

What I am here to do, though, is encourage you to think about them in a new context: as the paragons of a *frictionless* future, the most powerful drivers of our reconstituted relationships—both individual and collective—with time.

Does that sound complicated? It isn't.

Amazon and Apple sell us *stuff*.

Facebook and Google give us *information*.

What they all do is save us time, by reducing *friction*.

Amazon took all the friction out of retail, and then some. It used to be that if you wanted to buy something, you had to get up from your chair, walk out your door, go find it, buy it, and then bring it back home. These days, you don't even have to stand up, and the thing you want will be at your door a day or two later. Pretty much everyone who sells *anything* online is chasing Amazon's tail in one way or another, the result of which is that the time we used to spend finding and acquiring the material things we want or need is now ours to do with as we wish. That's profound.

How has Apple reduced friction? Instead of dragging ourselves out into the world, we now carry the world around with us in our pockets. They've even eliminated friction in the way we access that world—not with a push, but with a swipe. With a piece of hardware the size of a deck of cards, Apple took our lives and ironed out all the bumps, and allowed us to *glide* through so many of the things we do every day. Just consider Spotify, only made possible by the smartphone. Each and every one of us carries around a large part of all the music ever made in our pockets, with a lot less drag than if we had to bring it all on CD.

What has Facebook/Instagram done? They have made social interaction frictionless. Host that birthday party, post some pics of your kid, and you don't have to go visit grandma to keep her in the loop. Everybody already knows everybody's business thanks to Facebook/Instagram, which equals a lot of time saved.

And Google? (Or its parent company Alphabet, if you want to be nitpicky?) Google helped digitize our existence and made the transmission of information a *frictionless* process. Consider Duff's job as a journalist. It used to be that if he wanted to learn about something, he'd have to go to the library and interact with the Dewey decimal system. And the odds were good that he might not even find what he wanted. These days, much of the world's transmittable information is right there, in front of us, whenever we want it.

Yes, I know that each and every one of these companies has a lot to answer for. Amazon has destroyed as many businesses as it has helped create, and its track record with labor relations isn't exactly impressive. Apple has turned us into a civilization that walks around in a daze, head down, staring at our devices. Facebook has sold our identities right out from under us. And Google pretty much is holding all the world's information hostage. If you need to get a message out, you need to do it through them. You and all the purveyors of fake news and hate speech, who use both Google and YouTube to spread the ugly.

But none of that changes the fact of the matter that all four of these companies have changed human behavior, permanently. I don't think any of them actually set out with an explicit mission to reduce *friction*, but in doing so, and giving us back time, they have changed our behavior forever. Digital natives can't even comprehend a screen you can't swipe. Fifteen years ago, those screens didn't exist. The iPod was launched in 2001 and the iPhone in 2007. That was yesterday.

My main point is this: once they started us down this path, there was no turning back. With the result that today, humanity practically *demands* that the majority of the processes of our daily existence offer a reduction in *friction* if not the elimination of it entirely.

That's why the most forward-thinking entrepreneurs—more precisely, forward-thinking *people*—have recalibrated their ambition to helping others find those pockets of time that a reduction in friction provides.

Allow me to offer myself up as an example: I have two kids. Thanks to Jeff Bezos, I can't even imagine what my day-to-day would be like if I had to give back the hours I have saved to prepare for and execute a once-a-year event—a birthday party. The thought of that terrifies me.

You can find the "friction factor" in almost anything without much difficulty. It's about ease and cost/price and delivery time in consumer products. Thanks to Amazon, we now think that anything more than two days is an eternity. When I started The Inside, I had to abide by the ground rules set by Amazon, which literally changed the rules of consumption for most of humanity. If you want to succeed in retail these days, your only course of action is to figure out something that this gigantic thing called Amazon can't do that you can do in a more frictionless, designed, aspirational, and brand-worthy way. That's what Niraj did with Wayfair: he figured out frictionless in a big enough category—furniture—that it actually mattered.

Don't get me wrong: there has never been a time quite like today for small companies to challenge established monopolies. But here's the flip side of that argument: just as yesterday's incumbents have suddenly found themselves vulnerable to attacks from below, there are already *new* incumbents standing in the path of almost any company seeking to grow these days. And they are much more powerful than the incumbents of yesterday.

If you want to advertise today, you best be figuring out what to do with regard to the new incumbents. Pretty much all digital marketing takes place on Amazon, Facebook, Instagram, or Google Ads. Consumer brands used to spend their money in *People* magazine. That's no longer the case. In 2018, Google's share of digital ads was 41 percent, Facebook's 21 percent, and Amazon's 4 percent.[1]

It doesn't matter what a company wants to do, whether that's opening a coffee shop, trying to invent a new cancer drug, or consulting for big corporations on sustainability. Everyone has to ask themselves, "What is my strategy regarding these companies? Are they friend, foe, or neither?"

Let's talk a little more about Amazon in particular. Because in my business, they are an everyday concern and every single decision we make vis-à-vis competing and/or cooperating with Amazon will have a major influence on how we grow.

A binary split has emerged in online retail that makes the future look more straightforward than it has in years: Amazon owns anything basic, so if *you* want to own anything, it can't be basic. It doesn't matter what you make, whether it's fashion, furniture, homewares, electronics, shoes, or camping gear. If people are inclined to Google a product and do price comparisons, Amazon is almost always going to offer the lowest price. And unless you have some serious value-add to offer, Amazon will eventually come for you. They are a behemoth. Anyone who tries to compete with them directly is a fool. They've also got us by the throats: practically everyone is a Prime member, not just rich people; 68 percent of people with annual income below $100,000[2] are subscribers. (Those numbers are sure to rise even further, as the company announced in late April 2019 that it plans to start offering complimentary overnight shipping to Prime customers.)

Whatever it is you're selling, every single consumer business has to spend a large chunk of their time building moats against Amazon. That threat notwithstanding, there has been an explosion of new microbrands on the Internet, and The Inside intends to break out of that pack.

But we can't sit still. Before we know it, the Seattle juggernaut is going to be drop-shipping anything basic to our houses on a drone. In 2017, Amazon accounted for 70 percent of US e-commerce growth and nearly 35 percent of overall retail growth. And all of it at a lower cost than anyone else. You can't compete, but because of Amazon, *all* companies now require a relentless focus on *the need for speed.*

It used to be that the only people who cared about speed of delivery were pizza companies and pizza buyers. Today, if you can't get it where they want it, when they want it, you probably won't make the sale.

There is hope: only 5 percent of Prime subscribers report that Amazon is the only place they shop online.[3] (It's sort of amazing that 5 percent of them do, but that's another story.)

So let me repeat something I just said: the most important piece of advice I can offer fledgling entrepreneurs about this topic is so straightforward that it seems obvious, but that hasn't stopped a remarkable number of people—including me—from failing to do so: *Do Not Underestimate Amazon.*

How do you start a business competing against a company that doesn't need to make money on the sale? How do you innovate in a world where your competitor doesn't need to make money on the sale? I didn't face that challenge with Dwell-Studio. It wasn't exactly clear to me at Wayfair, either, because I was on the winning side of that equation. And while I now have a startup that is doing things that neither of those two can do, at the end of the day, we're all selling furniture.

At the same time, I love Amazon just as much as any other consumer. If I never had to go into a store again, I'd be fine. And you can't deny that Jeff Bezos has altered our experience of time in a wonderful way. He's given us pockets of time back, time that we don't spend at the grocery store or the toy store or Christmas shopping. That's why we love Amazon so much. Or at least that's why we *use* it as much as we do.

Now that I've told you that, I'm going to tell you that you also need to figure out how you're going to work with them—and Facebook and Google. Because if you don't, you're doomed. As a direct-to-consumer retailer, we are practically obligated to leverage Facebook and Google for customer acquisition. We advertise on both to reach our audience. They control digital advertising.

And you can't just wing it anymore; you need specialists. At The Inside, we hired a search engine optimization, or SEO, specialist, on a consulting basis to handle all the intricacies of the digital advertising universe. And it made a huge difference in our business—so much so that we are now in the market for a full-time specialist.

To those of us who were already in the workforce when these new positions were invented, it's still sometimes difficult to accept the necessity of them. Ten years ago, we all started hearing about "social media coordinators." And most of us thought, *That's not a real job*. Well, I've got news for you: it most certainly is. In September 2019, we poached one from L'Oréal.

The fact that jobs like social media coordinator and SEO specialist didn't exist ten years ago is one of the reasons we're writing this book. In my industry, both are hybrids that we couldn't even have conceived of a few years back—designers served with a side of technology savvy or data analytics. In other words, a left brain/right brain kind of person. Mark my words: that is *exactly* the kind of combination that every single employer will be searching for in the future—people capable of creative and collaborative problem-solving, who can move frictionlessly from their right brain to their left. If your kids have that inclination, you should help them develop it, as they will need it.

Even if you don't want to advertise on Facebook or Instagram or Pinterest, you have to be on Google. You can choose to not do these other things and try to grow organically, but it will be really slow. If you want to reach venture scale, you will be on all of them.

Do we sell on Amazon? We do not. At this point in time, their technology is not sophisticated enough to support the customization that we offer our customers. Not only that, we're in the direct-to-consumer business, and we're not sitting on enough margin to cut Amazon in on the sale. Amazon works when you have both retail and wholesale, and you sell to both channels. At The Inside, we pass all of our savings onto the consumer.

Do we advertise on Amazon? We do not. But we probably will, eventually. The last I heard, about 55 percent of people begin their product searches on Amazon. And those customers have what you call *high intent*. At this point, it makes more sense for us to put our advertising dollars on Facebook and Google and take a wait-and-see approach with Amazon. Two out of three ain't bad.

Long-term, I know I need to figure out a way to participate in Amazon Prime's ecosystem. It's one of the most elegant business models I've ever seen—they don't have customer acquisition costs! But I'm not going to be able to do that until I gain such efficiencies of scale that I might be able to share some of my profits with them. In the meantime, we will continue to use them as our office supply closet and hope they don't swallow us whole before we realize what's happening.

Chapter 4

A FRICTIONLESS EXPERIENCE

One of the things I've learned during my experience with
The Inside is that the things that drive an entrepreneur's
passion might not mean a damn thing to their customers. While
you need *your own* passion as a motivator, it's crucial to understand what motivates your customers too.

Allow me to elaborate: I'm in love with the whole supply chain
story. I thought my customers would be, too, but it turns out that
they couldn't care less. They just want a nice product that's inexpensive and arrives quickly—with zero *friction*. It might be important to me that there's transparency and sustainability in the
supply chain, but it's a rare customer who cares that much about
it themselves. (I'm not saying our customers don't care about
sustainability; I'm sure they do. But if they're talking about The
Inside, they're usually more interested in the price-quality-speed
trade-off than how we are doing our part to reduce waste by not
manufacturing our products until they've already been sold.)

What are the things that customers care about these days? I
just mentioned them, and they are the same things they've always

cared about: *Price and Quality and Speed*. Beyond that, though, there are a whole host of new considerations. The majority of customers these days want some sort of *Personalization*. They want the option of *Subscription*. They want to feel part of a community. And they want to talk to you directly. Rather, they want a direct line of communication to the company, usually via text or email. (Phone calls are an endangered species.) Put all that under the heading *Direct-to-Consumer*.

Brick-and-mortar isn't what it used to be. If for some reason you require further proof, consider the fact that in 2017, Lord & Taylor sold its flagship Italian Renaissance building in New York City to WeWork. One of Fifth Avenue's most beautiful buildings was worth more as a rent-an-office than as a department store.

That's not to say that today's customers don't still identify with particular brands. They most certainly do. The idea that there's a *community* that contains companies and their customers has staked out serious claim in the public vernacular of late. (I'm not saying it's a new thing, just that the term has gone viral.)

There's a weird disconnect at play here: we are holding bad corporate actors to higher and higher ethical standards than at any time in memory. And yet we will let them seduce us with the idea that a company isn't simply a legal structure, but something resembling an actual human being. You can send "them" a text. Who is them? Who do you love?

Pop Quiz: Who said the following?

"[It's necessary] to make the people understand and love the company. Not merely to be consciously dependent on it—not merely to regard it as a necessity—not merely to take it for granted—but to love it—to hold real affection for it."[1]

Answers:

(A) A "performance marketer"

(B) The publicity people from luggage—er, *travel*—company Away

(C) The public relations department for the Fyre Festival

(D) Someone from AT&T during the dawn of "new capitalism," more than one hundred years ago

Answer: D

Plus ça change, plus c'est la même chose.

A recent story in the *New York Times* gave us the news that "[A]ll kinds of companies are trying the strategy of using emotion and 'shared values' to build relationships with consumers—and to sell them more stuff."[2]

Of course, not everyone can stop themselves from going overboard.

Adam Neumann of WeWork thought his office-space rental company would drive down suicide rates because "no one ever feels alone." The company's IPO prospectus mentioned the word "community" more than 150 times.

Christopher Brandt, the chief marketing officer of Chipotle, said the following during an earnings call not too long ago: "Our ultimate marketing mission is to make Chipotle not just a food brand but a purpose-driven lifestyle brand."[3] Yes, you read that right. Chipotle is a purpose-driven lifestyle brand.

Likewise Brad Dickerson, the CEO of meal-kit company Blue Apron, is in search of a "deeper connection with consumers" and describes the company as "a strong consumer lifestyle brand that reinforces our identity—to not simply be a transactional e-commerce business, but play a more meaningful role in our customers' lives."[4] Uh . . . okay.

Finally, Lululemon has "a vision to be the experiential brand that ignites a community of people living the sweatlife through sweat, grow, and connect." Sweatlife, you say?

Anyway, I'm getting ahead of myself. Because before you can build a community, you've got to acquire a customer. The Holy Grail is to figure out how to keep that customer. I'm talking about two sides of the most important coin in retail: *customer acquisition* and *retention*.

At DwellStudio, I had almost zero visibility into my customers. And one of the most surprising things I learned at Wayfair, in fact, was just *how little I knew about them.* I mean, I knew that I didn't know a whole lot—when you're selling primarily via wholesale, your ultimate retail customer is once removed—yet I nevertheless thought I knew enough to walk into work each day and set about designing for them. But then came Wayfair, and . . . *all that data.*

The then global head of Wayfair's Algorithms & Analytics was the first person to show me how data could be represented in 3-D—literally, inside a cube. The team is all MIT data scientists, so I guess a rotating cube of data made perfect sense to them. Me? I could barely read an Excel spreadsheet at that point. But I was a fast learner, and before long, I started seeing things in that data that others at Wayfair probably weren't even looking for.

Wayfair is a marketplace—you see something, and you buy it—and they are masters at understanding how products sell online. Start adding design elements, though, and it becomes more difficult to tease out just *why* something is selling: Is it the design or the photography? Or the price? Millennial buyers were just beginning to come into their own, and I suddenly realized that I had access to the best possible data one could ask for if you wanted to get out in front of the next generation's spending habits in the realm of home furnishings. Those cubes of data were a window into the future itself.

Part of that future is this: As technology becomes better and online commerce is forced to be more nuanced, both AR (augmented reality) and VR (virtual reality) will become larger parts of the customer experience. Companies will have to be more inspirational, providing content and transacting in a much different—and more robust—way. Our customers can customize and design on our website; we try to inspire them too.

In 2020, customers not only want a *frictionless* experience, they also want you to know what they want without having to spell it out for you. The companies in the following profiles are streamlining every part of that experience.

We start with Eric Kinariwala at Capsule, and his mission to take the pain out of pharmacy visits. David Greenberg is doing the same with the hassle of moving. We follow those with a handful of entrepreneurs who have taken out the middlemen and given their customers what they want when they want it, whether that's women's razors (Billie), athleisure wear (Vuori), custom-formulated shampoo (Prose), or men's skincare (Geologie). Next up: one of the greatest examples of how to succeed in the shadow of Amazon, Robert Wang's Instant Pot. And we close out the chapter with two companies that are doing things that simply couldn't be done before the digitization of commerce, Policygenius and Bluecore.

The End of the Line

ERIC KINARIWALA, FOUNDER AND CEO OF CAPSULE

Has anyone been able to dodge the exquisite pain of the friction in the doctor-prescription-patient-pharmacy supply chain? We think not. Eric Kinariwala wants to take our pain away.

In January 2015, Eric Kinariwala woke up in his apartment on Manhattan's Lower East Side with a throbbing headache. He called his doctor and told him it felt like his head was going to explode. After asking a couple of questions, the doctor concluded that it was most likely a sinus infection, and told Kinariwala that he'd call a prescription for a five-day antibiotic Z-Pak into the closest Duane Reade pharmacy. *There, problem solved.*

Not so fast. "When I walked into the store, literally everything that could go wrong with the pharmacy went wrong for me," he says. After walking down a broken escalator into the store's "dark, dingy basement," with zero cell phone reception, Kinariwala then stood in line for almost an hour, only to be told upon reaching the front of the line that the pharmacy didn't have any Z-Paks. *In January.* Deflated but not defeated, he figured he'd call his doctor back and ask him to call the prescription into another local pharmacy. But his phone had died searching for a signal in that Duane Reade basement. *Problem still not solved.*

Kinariwala eventually got his prescription. But the experience grated on him. In the first part of his career, he'd worked for an institutional investor, analyzing companies in retail, health care, and technology, among other things. He didn't realize it at the time, but all of those specialties were going to come together in what followed.

"I woke up the next morning and thought, *How did I just waste an hour and a half without getting the medication I needed?*" he says. "From an industry that practically has an outpost on every street corner in America?"

The analyst in him took over. What he found surprised him: there are 70,000 pharmacies in America, making it the second largest category of retail in the nation—with some $350 billion in annual sales. "I'd never thought about it this way either," he says. "But the pharmacy is the most frequent interaction people have with the health-care industry—it's the thing you do more than anything else, including visiting your doctor, going to the hospital, or dealing with your insurance company. It's the heartbeat of health care, so to speak."

We all know how the system works: a pharmaceutical company makes a drug, your doctor writes you a prescription for it, the pharmacy dispenses it, your insurance company pays for some part of it, you pay for the rest, and you take it. All of the above stakeholders come together to make "pharmacy" work. But, as Kinariwala's own experience points out, that doesn't always happen as smoothly as we'd like. "Not only that," he adds, "no one had been thinking about better ways of bringing them all together where there's value for them in sharing data and working together to create better health-care outcomes." That's when he decided to found Capsule, *to solve the problem himself.*

Capsule is an online pharmacy that delivers prescriptions straight to New Yorkers' doors. Doctors can send a prescription to Capsule just as easily as they send one to Duane Reade or CVS. The company employs real-life pharmacists ready to chat with you about your prescriptions. They take care of refills automatically. And they scour the Internet for coupons from drug companies and other deals, so you get the best possible price. Meaning, you get it at the same or a better price than you'd pay after waiting in line at your pharmacy.

Not only that, you don't have to wait around only to find that your brick-and-mortar pharmacy is out of stock. According to Kinariwala, 40 percent of pharmacy visits are a waste of time—they're out of stock. That's partly because if you're going to have a pharmacy on every corner, you can't stock everything in every one of them, so the business model of the pharmacy chains practically requires that they are generally out of stock of many medications. But the other reason is that the pharmacy chains never even bothered to do what many tech-forward consumer goods companies are doing nowadays, which is predictive inventory for those customers who are *definitely* going to be needing their medication again next month. "You'd be amazed at how many diabetics have told us that they inject the exact same amount of insulin every day, and run out the same day every month, and yet their pharmacy is always out of stock," says Kinariwala. "That's insane to me."

What's more, predictive inventory should help Capsule manage its own business better than the competition can. Consider the following: CVS acquired Aetna in 2018 in a deal worth nearly $70 billion. But the combined entity swung to a loss of $421 million in the fourth quarter of 2018, down from a profit of $3.29 billion the year before.[5] Whatever is going on in that company, there is variance and unpredictability to its results. That's what Kinariwala is looking to eliminate.

Are the chain pharmacies concerned about this new upstart? In a

two-week period in early 2019, CVS announced that it would hence-
forth offer delivery and promised to scour the web for coupons and
savings. *Problems are being solved.*

Kinariwala has bigger plans than eliminating the need to wait in line
for your prescriptions, though. If the pharmacy is our primary source of
interaction with the health-care industry, he says, then it's possible to
view it as the "connective tissue" between the industry's various stakeholders. Gather the right data, he adds, and "the pharmacy should be
your single source of truth for all of health care."

Can any one company do that? Convince all the stakeholders in a
trillion-dollar industry to use it as the central repository? Doubtful. But
Kinariwala says he doesn't have to do that. He just needs to operate
like Slack, which, by integrating with the likes of Google and Dropbox,
has begun to emerge as the platform that sits at the heart of so many
office workers' lives. Kinariwala won't call Capsule the Slack of health
care, but we will.

"Take all the information that's in silos," says Kinariwala. "Drug companies have some that they share and some that they don't, so do hos-
pitals, so do doctors. Imagine a world where all those people decided
to combine that data. What kinds of powerful things could happen in
terms of better health care for all?"

Backing up to the simple pharmacy part: Kinariwala refers to Capsule as an "iceberg" business—the kind where the consumer, using the
company's app, might confuse the ease of use for simplicity of technology. The fact is, there's a lot of technology that's underwater powering
all that. "I'm a big admirer of Wayfair in terms of all the proprietary
systems they build on the back end to handle the logistics of selling
large pieces of furniture," he says.

The best way to think of companies like Capsule, Wayfair, or The
Inside is to think of them as technology companies. That's why a

venture investor like Thrive Capital, which also backed Oscar, a technology-focused health insurance company, is one of Capsule's own backers. Both companies are attacking inefficient parts of the health-care space, and are using technology to do so.

Is Amazon coming for Capsule? Kinariwala says he has no idea, but we do know that with the June 2018 acquisition of mail-order pharmacy PillPack, Jeff Bezos sent a shot across the bow of the entire health-care industry in the same way that Capsule has in New York. For now, Capsule has the edge in same-day, hand-delivery of prescriptions—for many drugs, it's still mandatory that the consumer show identification, and Capsule's team of delivery people are trained at checking IDs and taking signatures in a way that Amazon isn't in a position to do.

That brings us to one of the more salient aspects of Capsule's business. Along with their delivery team, the company also employs pharmacists that customers can text in real time, asking questions about their prescriptions or otherwise. It's what makes Capsule part of what Kinariwala calls the third wave of e-commerce.

The first wave was commodity products, and the winner has been Amazon. Amazon has perfected the delivery of everyday items. And you don't need to interact with anyone to get that done.

The second wave includes companies like Casper and Warby Parker, companies that took relatively generic products and put emotionally engaging brands on top of them. Here, too, there is no real need for human intervention to make the sale.

The third wave will be those companies that bring a service, or human component, into the model. The ones that will succeed next will have to do something like putting a real-life pharmacist inside your phone for you, as Capsule has done.

"You don't want to be selling things like the mugs, markers, or dry erasers that we bought on Amazon for our office," says Kinariwala. "What you want is to be in a business where there's a human required, and the three largest of those are health care, real estate, and financial services."

The chief pharmacist at Capsule is an old friend of Kinariwala's, Sonia Patel, who came on board early to build out the concept with him. The two of them knew they were onto something not two or three months after they opened their doors in New York in May 2016. One evening at around eight, a text came in from a customer saying, "Hey Sonia, can I take iron supplements while I'm pregnant?" After a back-and-forth, the customer added, "By the way, is it weird that you're the first person I'm telling I'm pregnant? My husband doesn't even know." Contrary to what you might expect from an e-commerce brand, Capsule hadn't *removed* the human component from the transaction; they'd actually brought it to the fore, giving their customer the opportunity to ask a *very* personal question in the way they wanted in a way that felt private and secure. "That was the moment for us," he says. And probably just the first of many more to come.

The One-Click Move

DAVID GREENBERG, FOUNDER AND CEO OF UPDATER

Nobody likes moving. There's the move itself, and then there's the paper-work. David Greenberg of Updater won't move your stuff for you, but his company will move everything else, including your insurance coverage, cable provider, utilities, and more. Updater removes most of the friction from one of life's unavoidable aggravations.

The best ideas for new businesses are usually those that solve real prob-lems for real people. It has always been thus. You can get into some really big numbers really fast if you manage to dislodge an incumbent that's been abusing a position of privilege—think Blockbuster, which had so abused its own customers that when Netflix offered DVD rentals with *no late fees*, Blockbuster almost collapsed overnight. But you don't have to dislodge an existing company to solve real problems. Some people conjure their white space right out of thin air. Consider the case of David Greenberg of Updater.

In his previous life as a mergers and acquisitions lawyer at white-shoe law firm Cravath, Swaine & Moore in New York, Greenberg ran up against a headache that most of us have faced: the logistical nightmare known as moving.

As so many of us have done, he made a list of all the things he needed to do before his move, such as all the businesses he needed to contact, including utilities, cable company, moving company, storage company, credit card companies, his bank, and more. "I called it my *update list*," he says. In the midst of complaining to friends about how much effort it was taking—and how much *friction* it entailed—Greenberg heard himself saying, "Everybody moves, and everybody hates the experience. Someday, someone is going to start a technology company that completely and efficiently reinvents how people move. And everybody is going to love it."

Greenberg didn't know exactly what that technology platform would look like, but he knew that it was an area ripe for innovation: technology hadn't really made a dent in the relocation industry. What if, he asked, all you had to do was enter in where you were moving, and the technology took care of everything else for you, including changing your cable company, switching your address with the local utility, and even going so far as to recommend things like dry cleaners in your new neighborhood? Why on earth wouldn't people want that? Why indeed?

When someone challenged him with the line so many entrepreneurs have heard—"If you think it's such a good idea, why don't *you* do it?"—he surprised himself by following through on the suggestion. It was 2009, in the midst of the financial crisis, and he quit his comfortable job as a corporate lawyer to start Updater. "People thought I was crazy," he says. Welcome to the club, David.

The initial idea was just the consumer value proposition. Before long, though, Greenberg realized that he was targeting a really interesting moment in people's lives from a marketer's standpoint. "People make all sorts of key spending decisions when they move," he says. "Their brand loyalties are really vulnerable at that exact moment."

This is one of those start-up ideas that makes sense intuitively, but ends up being a nightmare from an execution standpoint. Imagine trying to make cable companies behave better. Who the hell would take on that task?

Someone who's very stubborn. "In other aspects of life, being stubborn might not be such a great thing," says Greenberg, "but for an entrepreneur, it's great. You just keep pushing through and block out the sound of 'This isn't working.' There's the other voice inside you that's saying, irrationally, 'No, no, no, it's going to work.'" It's at this point in the interview that I realize Greenberg is a kindred spirit—the delusion, the optimism, the delusional optimism, the refusal to fail.

I ask him if he can point to a couple of mistakes he wouldn't make the next time around. "That's easy," he replies.

For starters, he didn't hire a cofounder. "I was not a technologist, and instead of finding a technology partner, I hired the cheapest engineers I could find on Craigslist, which might be the worst idea ever," he says. He also spent a lot of time on intellectual property protection—he had a lawyer's instinct to try and protect his ideas—but realizes now he should have been sharing them with everybody and getting as much feedback as possible, so that he could iterate as quickly as possible. "I had all the wrong instincts at first," he says. "I should have been finding partners and sharing, but I was operating alone, keeping the ideas to myself and trying to build it myself in an environment that I controlled. Needless to say, in the first year or two we didn't get very far."

(I empathize with his instincts. When I started DwellStudio, I didn't trademark it, nationally or internationally. Why? Because I hadn't realized that I should. I couldn't afford to copyright my designs either. And what do you know, a giant competitor swooped in and stole a huge chunk of my business. Not only that, someone in the UK jacked my entire company, logo included, and launched over there.)

Greenberg says he won't make those mistakes again, but he's also quite sure there isn't going to be a next time—he's happy at Updater. "I like being the CEO of this later-stage company," he says. "A sane person would have quit one hundred times in the first two or three years of Updater. We got turned down by fifty-plus venture capital investors."

That's not a problem anymore. Today, Greenberg has a classic mix of investors. His first serious backer was someone he met at a wedding—a stranger who happened to have enough time to hear the Updater story and really get it. Following that, heavyweights like Soft-Bank and IA Ventures came in. A strategic investment from the National Association of Realtors followed. The company had an initial public offering in Australia (that first investor was Australian), which brought in Fidelity Investments, but last year, he took it private again. Why go private? Because the US-based venture capital community finally wrapped their heads around the idea, and began voicing interest in a large late-stage acceleration growth round. It's not like the numbers aren't there: when Updater went public, it had a 2 percent market share in the United States. Today, about 20 percent of *all moves* in the country are being sent onto its platform.

And today, a user can hire a moving company with *one click*. They can transfer their utilities with *one click*. All sorts of companies, from insurance companies to dry cleaners, have asked how to get on the platform. Updater provides them with an API so they can send in special promotions and deals that are then distributed electronically to the relevant people who are moving. The service is free for actual consumers, and Updater is paid by its real estate partners as well as the service providers who want access to the platform. On the real estate partner side, Updater has boasted a ridiculous 99 percent retention rate over the last several years.

Sometimes, it's expensive to acquire customers. But sometimes, it's not. When it comes to the people who are actually moving, real estate companies *pay Updater* to offer the service. The people moving love it, it helps real estate firms both save money and generate new revenues, and real estate brokers love it because it helps with referrals and client retention. This is what's known as a B2B2C business model.

It all sounds so . . . *frictionless.* "Our strategy has changed a ton over the past eight years, but the vision hasn't changed at all," says Greenberg. "We wanted to take a formerly painful process and turn it into something that's enjoyable, that takes a few clicks on your phone. No friction whatsoever." The problem with relocation is that you need a frictionless experience across fifteen different verticals, because there are so many things you need to do—insurance, cable, utility, the move itself, truck rental.

And here's the best part: this is one of those situations where a dominant brand might actually be good for consumers. "If we can aggregate a large enough percentage of all household moves onto one platform," says Greenberg, "then we will have the leverage to convince businesses to integrate their purchasing or sign-up experience into Updater. We're coming close to an inflection point where if those service providers *aren't* on Updater, it's going to be problematic for them."

Greenberg is obviously on to something. Nobody wants to deal with anything anymore. They just want to click once and have it be done. Updater's real estate partners get this, and have signed on in droves. Service providers, on the other hand—cable companies, in particular—are more reluctant, because they want to own the customer. "The problem is that they're not incentivized to give users a full view of the market and help them make great choices, and they focus on just the one vertical that they operate. None of them has the ability to build a frictionless and unbiased experience across multiple verticals," says Greenberg. "They deliver a very high-friction experience."

Today, Updater partners with thousands of real estate brokers and buildings around the country. They have about one thousand corporate partnerships with big property management and real estate brokerage firms. Updater integrates into their back-end software, the real estate firms send Updater a feed of residents who are moving, and then Updater sends them personalized invites to the branded version of the app that's been customized for the real estate partner. How many invites are we talking about? Millions of households a year.

When we ask him about competition, Greenberg says, point blank, that there isn't any. Updater has 20 percent of the market, and nobody else even has 0.05 percent. As with many great start-up ideas, what Updater is competing against is the status quo. "It would be good for us if another platform did get some scale, because we could learn from things they do well and maybe even join forces with them," he says. "Right now, we are the only relo-tech platform with any national scale." Proving that while you may be able to take the M&A lawyer out of the law firm, you can't take the M&A out of the lawyer.

Project Body Hair

GEORGINA GOOLEY, COFOUNDER OF BILLIE

For decades, women have paid a "pink tax" on products—including razors—that are practically interchangeable with those sold to men. Georgina Gooley found that offensive and rewrote the narrative. She took the friction out of the story, the product, and the price.

It was probably inevitable that we'd end up talking to a company that makes razors in a book called *Frictionless*. It wasn't that long ago that two companies blazed new trails in men's subscription shaving services—Harry's and Dollar Shave Club. But the story we tell in this book is of female-first shaving and body brand Billie, and its cofounders Georgina Gooley and Jason Bravman.

Gooley hails from a branding and marketing background. Bravman worked in finance. Both had been wondering why razor companies were always focused on male consumers. What's more, both had noticed that women's razors were subject to the "pink tax"—the extra 7 percent or so that women are sometimes charged for certain goods and services, for no good reason.

When they were introduced by a mutual friend, the idea clicked.

"We wanted to create a company that puts women first," says Gooley, "first by giving them a product that's designed for the way they shave, and then priced in line with the affordable men's razor subscriptions, eliminating the pink tax in the process."

Why, you might ask, have women and men largely used the same razors, when the differences between how—and what—they shave are so legion? Men shave in front of a sink; women tend to shave in the shower. Men shave their face; women shave ten times the surface area that men do. Billie's blades—five of them at once—come encased in shave soap, which provides extra lubrication. The cartridges themselves are rounded, because women shave in tighter areas and need to turn corners in armpits and elsewhere.

None of that is revolutionary, mind you.

What was?

1. Gooley and Bravman decided that Billie customers weren't going to be charged an extra 7 percent just because they were women.
2. They decided to literally change the narrative around women and shaving.

How so? When she researched the space, Gooley discovered that about one hundred years ago, in 1915, American women were first told, through a mass marketing channel, that they should remove their objectionable hair. The selling tactic, in other words, was to make them feel ashamed of their hair. While the tactics shifted over the subsequent century, the idea that hair on various parts of the female body is offensive did not.

Consider any commercial or print advertisement you've ever seen for women's razors. In the commercials, pay attention: it's women shaving *shaved legs—there is no hair.* "Hair was so taboo in that context that they couldn't even show a proper product demonstration," says Gooley.

(When Jeff Raider of Harry's decided to move into women's razors himself, he cited a similar anachronism, of typical women's shaving products showing women "walking through waterfalls" on the packaging.)

So Billie started Project Body Hair, which had a two-fold objective. First, it would show that, yes, women do have body hair. Second, it would suggest that shaving was not an expectation but a *choice*, making it the first-ever razor company to do so. "We don't have the authority to tell you whether you should shave or not—it's a personal choice," says Gooley. "But if you do choose to shave, we've got a great razor for you."

The project launched in June 2018 with the tag line, "A celebration of female body hair . . . wherever it is or isn't." The campaign showed female body hair for the first time ever in razor ads, with both video and print assets that showed body hair on models in a beautiful light. Since then, the video has been viewed more than 22 million times and covered by media in twenty-three countries. Within a few months, the largest brands (and newer challengers) jumped on board and started to show hair being shaved in their own commercials as well. The narrative, it seems clear, has been changed—for the better.

What has that meant for Billie's business? The company raised $1.5 million from family and friends to launch in November 2017. By day two of operations, they'd sold to all fifty states. By month four, they'd reached their twelve-month goals. They sold out of razors more than once in 2018, and investors were soon clamoring to get on board—via a $10 million seed round in April 2018 and a $25 million Series A round in January 2019.

Like most direct-to-consumer subscription brands these days, Billie finds most of its customers on social media. And because it is in direct discussion with those customers (unlike, say, the number one incumbent competitor . . . cough, *Gillette*, cough), Billie can react more quickly to customer feedback and seems poised to take a big bite out of the $1.2 to $1.5 billion market for women's shaving in the United States.

One way it's going to do that is to send razors to women on a schedule that customers set themselves—every one, two, or three months. They also offer customer service seven days a week, which means that if you need your new razors sent out tomorrow, all you've got to do is send them a text. That, or email. There's *frictionlessness* here too—you don't need to call an annoying 1–800 number and wait in line; you just send them a text and you're done.

In an interview with LinkedIn founder Reid Hoffman, entrepreneurial legend Barry Diller said that, "I think the best thing you can ever have is a clean piece of paper. You know? So you've got a clean piece of paper, and in the truest sense of clean. Meaning, nothing is sacred—you get to just start."

When it comes to Billie, that's what happened. Gooley started with a fresh piece of paper by going direct-to-consumer and avoiding what would surely be a futile fight with the likes of Gillette in retail merchandising. But she followed that with going political, like another of our featured entrepreneurs, Alexandra Fine (see page 000). Razors for women have clearly, and forever, been made by men. By including the customer in the dialogue, and by telling them that their body—including the hair on it—was their own, to do with what they will, Gooley and Bravman put another shovelful of dirt on the grave of patriarchal selling, advertising, and dialogue.

The Most Comfortable Pair
of Sweatpants Ever Made

JOE KUDLA, FOUNDER AND CEO OF VUORI

Joe Kudla and his startup Vuori gave active men (and women) something they didn't even know they were missing: a frictionless transition from the beach to the coffee shop to the office. Vuori's day-to-night athleisure wear isn't just stylish; it's some of the most comfortable clothing ever made.

Joe Kudla has always been a very active person, from his youth in Washington State to playing lacrosse for the University of San Diego, where he majored in accounting. He says he beat up his body playing sports, but that didn't stop him from a brief career as a model after graduation. His friends still tease him about it, but they're working with the material at hand; after modeling, he joined Ernst & Young as a CPA—hardly the stuff of endless jokes.

The entrepreneurial urge came on pretty quickly, though, and he left E&Y at the tender age of twenty-five to cofound a startup that sought to help companies deal with compliance issues in the post-Enron, Sarbanes-Oxley environment. The company grew to about 120 people over the course of a decade, but it was never enough to satisfy the left side of Kudla's brain, the one that wanted to design clothing and work with artists and other creatives. When he wasn't analyzing financial statements, Kudla was shopping fabrics with jobbers in Los Angeles, going to dye houses and cut-and-sew houses, and hustling small batches of garments to specialty boutiques.

The way things were going, he was destined to have a corporate day job and a weekend hobby in apparel. He was also destined, from what he could tell, for a lifetime of pain: Kudla's sports history and overall active lifestyle had left him with a bad back. And then fate intervened: sometime around 2008, he decided that he needed to do something "restorative" for his body—that's when he discovered yoga.

"I really fell in love with the practice," he says. What he didn't fall in love with was the available yoga apparel for men. "Lululemon was primarily focused on the female consumer," he says, "and there weren't a lot of options for guys." For would-be entrepreneurs in search of their own "aha moment," this is what they look and sound like.

He ran a few numbers. First, as a surfer, he knew that there were about 4 million surfers in the United States. Second, there were 30 million people practicing yoga, some 30 percent of which were men. If they made stuff for both, they'd be bigger than a dedicated yoga brand, with a total market maybe two or three times the size of surfing brands. Kudla could name twenty surfing brands off the top of his head, but not a single male-focused yoga-and-surf brand.

And then he brought everything back to his own personal experience. "I grew up wearing Nike and Under Armour," he says, "but as a thirty-year-old, my priorities had changed. I wasn't looking to be the next Tom Brady anymore—that dream has sadly died and I was not relating as well to the ultra-competitive messages and the logo-driven products typical of the mainstream active brands. By then my primary motivations were staying healthy, keeping up with my kids, and having fun doing the things I love. Today I want my clothing to not only be really comfortable and perform well but to work across a lot of different pursuits typical of a dynamic modern life, both in and out of the gym. We boiled it down to its simplest form and made products for our friends and community and figured we'd see where it went from there."

Why didn't he just buy some Lululemon men's apparel and be done with it? "I have nothing but respect for them," says Kudla. "They created the premium active category and I am forever indebted to them. But it always felt like my wife's brand to me. And I don't think I'm alone in not feeling that comfortable going into a Lululemon store and shopping. Although, hey—they could be a billion-dollar men's brand in a couple of years, so who am I to judge?"

And so he set out to create a new active apparel brand for men. Vuori isn't just about yoga. It's all things California—surfing, yoga, hiking, and the like. Based in Encinitas, which is just outside San Diego, it also draws more inspiration from the urban street culture than the typical male athletic brand. It's summarized best by Kudla himself: "We wanted an aesthetic that delivered on our brand promise of versatility—you can wear it to the gym, to yoga, out on a trail run, or chasing your kids around the house, but it works equally well when you're meeting a friend for a drink afterward," he says. Duff loves the stuff and says the reason is simple: in a fashion moment that seems obsessed with catering to the little boys of Brooklyn, Kudla is making clothing for men.

In keeping with the historical moment, as well as a desire to have a direct relationship with his customers, Kudla launched Vuori as a digitally native brand. "We started building it one day at a time through Facebook advertising," he says. "There was a little bit of marketing to fitness and yoga instructors as well, but it was predominantly social media." Kudla admits being a little shocked at what you can do with a couple of good designers, a bit of money to spend on marketing, and the Internet: "It's funny . . . actually, it's amazing what you can do with a laptop and a cell phone," he says.

At first, it was all Facebook, but after the acquisition of Instagram, Vuori now works with the company to optimize to the best audiences served across their network, which now includes Instagram. Trust us, this works. Duff, who Vuori reached through Facebook, might be one of their best customers. He owns countless pairs of yoga shorts, yoga shirts, board shorts, casual shorts, hoodies, and more. And he is firmly of the opinion that Vuori sells the most comfortable pair of sweatpants ever made.

But times have changed since 2008. Facebook advertising has gotten a lot more expensive. The digital space has gotten a lot more crowded. These days, Vuori still uses social media, but its media and marketing strategies have transcended it, and now include podcast advertising as well as direct mail and catalogs.

However, here's the thing: you can talk about digital channels and marketing until you're blue in the face, but if your product quality is anything short of excellent, it won't really matter in the end. "Customer acquisition only works if you have great products and you're not going to have a huge return rate and poor reviews," says Kudla.

Kudla is so confident in the quality of Vuori products, in fact, that he will not subsidize potential repeat business by giving away the first purchase at a loss. "We have always sought profitability on first purchase as a discipline," he says. Kudla only raised $2.6 million to launch Vuori, and while he won't reveal top-line results, he does say that he has more than a few competitors that have raised ten to twenty times as much and spent a lot of it on aggressive marketing, all without reaching Vuori's more organically driven growth. Kudla isn't telling, but the company's revenues for 2018 were estimated between $30 million and $50 million.

How do they stay on top of customer wants and tastes? By leveraging the technological tools available to anyone working in apparel today. The same way that I view The Inside as essentially a technology company that sells furniture, Kudla sees himself as a bit of a technologist himself. Or at least as someone who hires them.

"We look for technology sensibilities in every job candidate because it's so pervasive in everything that we do," he says. The old model of wholesale—make samples, get them into your reps' hands, have them go out and sell, turn in their orders, produce them, ship them to a retailer, and hope they sell—is archaic. Today, technology has invaded every part of that process, from line planning to presales planning to communication with the sales force. Reps manage their own orders within Vuori's technology environment, which has implications for everything from enterprise resource planning (ERP) to fulfillment. Everything including the most arcane, antiquated aspects of running an apparel business has become more efficient through the use of technology. Instead of bringing on different technical resources that can service each different function of the business, Vuori has built something akin to an in-house technology agency that services all of the different function areas of the business at once.

But the integration isn't just internal. It knits together the three main ways Vuori sells as well—e-commerce, wholesale, and retail. "We're finding great, integrated technologies that help us across all the channels," says Kudla. "When you get cross-channel visibility, you can make way smarter decisions." What does he mean by that? He means that if a customer buys a product from REI or Nordstrom, they want to be able to come into one of Vuori's retail stores and return it. They can already do that at retail giants like West Elm. But at a startup that's only raised $2.5 million? "I would say that's the startup's challenge, regardless of how well you're capitalized," says Kudla. "How do you make yourself competitive from a customer experience standpoint?"

To this point, Kudla has avoided selling on Amazon. Why? For a couple of reasons. One, he wants to own the customer relationship. Two, when Amazon makes decisions—cutting prices, putting in a big order—it can dramatically impact the business. "It's a bit scary to be in a business relationship where you have very little control over how your products are priced and who the actual sellers of your product are," he says. "Until there is more control and transparency, we are choosing to focus on other channels of distribution." Of course, there's also the fact that Vuori already has all the growth it can handle servicing the channels it already works with. That's a good place to be.

In the meantime, Kudla is using what he has learned in yoga to help him navigate the ups and downs of entrepreneurship. "I consider myself a fairly self-aware person," he says. "And as someone who's really devoted himself to the practice of yoga and meditation, I have found both useful as I go through the experiences of building this company. Because business, and entrepreneurship especially, is just a lot like life—you have your ups, your downs, your moments of elation, and your moments of being completely scared. I just try to take the middle path, keep up the positive momentum, and breathe through it all—the good times are great in the moment, but they will pass and so will the bad. So I try to keep that perspective with me." Namaste.

Getting Personal

ARNAUD PLAS, COFOUNDER AND CEO OF PROSE

Personalization is the express train to a frictionless existence. Arnaud Plas and his colleagues at Prose are harnessing technology to sell you something (in their case, shampoo) that is yours and yours alone. Forget about wasting money on products you might end up not needing—it's made to your exact specifications and arrives every month like clockwork.

When I launched The Inside, it might have looked like I was launching another home furnishings brand, à la DwellStudio. But, as I mentioned previously, what I was really doing was launching a technology company that just happens to make home furnishings. If you're going to offer customers the ability to mix and match, to choose everything from which fabrics to which legs they want, and the ability to mix it all together into something that's very personal while still being scalable from a manufacturing point of view, then you're running a technology company.

But it's a different kind of "technology" than that which brought us the Industrial Revolution. That brought us manufacturing at scale, the mechanization of everything, and an absurd level of standardization and sorting of everything from products to people. But that whole model has started coming apart. Customers don't want to be sorted anymore; they want you to make something *just for them.*

Arnaud Plas of Prose has used the tools of modern e-commerce— one-to-one connections with customers via a proprietary platform, manufacture on demand, and proprietary algorithms—to do something no major cosmetics company could ever think of doing: custom-make shampoo for each and every customer, all the way down to the label on the bottle.

"When we first pitched investors," says Plas, "more than a few of them told us, 'We don't invest in shampoo.' And what I kept replying was, 'I don't think you get what we're doing here. We're not a shampoo company. We're transforming the beauty industry through technology.' The ones that didn't invest at first are all calling me now and asking how to fix their mistake."

Plas likes to point out that Prose isn't just the future; it's also the past. "Two hundred years ago, the apothecary made you a special shampoo," he says. "But then the Industrial Revolution came along and we decided to make one shampoo for everyone." In the early 1900s, the innovator Helena Rubinstein, inventor of cosmetology, started to open things up again when she segmented skin into dry, oily, and normal. And then things got out of hand. Today, there are a thousand shampoos on store shelves broken down into broad stereotypes that don't fit *any* specific woman whatsoever.

Prose gets personal by asking you to answer twenty-five questions— about your hair, your scalp, your lifestyle, the climate in which you live, your preferred fragrances—and then Plas and his colleagues concoct your unique formulation, drawing from seventy-five naturally active in- gredients. "We have chemists, data scientists, developers, and project managers working together," he says. "That could not have happened at L'Oréal."

How does he know that? Because that's where he used to work, ironically doing product innovation. But it was a different kind of innovation than that which he's practicing today. "We'd make millions of units of a product and put it on all the shelves in the United States or France," he says. "A year or two later, we'd take half of it back because we had a new 'innovation' coming. Retailers demanded it, saying, 'If you don't innovate, I will give the shelf space to someone else.' But it wasn't real innovation. Sometimes, consumer tests would come back with poor marks, but we'd be so far along we'd push it through anyway."

So how unique is unique? Do the math on the ingredients and dosages, and you quickly get to about 50 billion possible combinations. In the first ten months of 2018, Prose shipped 35,000 unique formulations to customers.

What gave him the courage to compete against not just his former employer but every other gigantic brand in personal care? "Well, I think it's pretty obvious today that what used to be their strength is now their weakness," he says. "Being a large company with tons of specific employees and multiple brands relying on the same R & D—that's a weakness."

The team at Prose had already changed their formulation algorithm twenty-five times by the time we met Plas in late 2018. An early anti-dandruff ingredient from the pomegranate peel, for example, created a dark red/brown color that customers didn't like, so they changed ingredients. The switch only took two months. He can't even imagine trying to pull that off at L'Oréal, where a new product launch takes between seven and ten *years* from new molecule to new product on shelves. Talk about removing friction from an antiquated process!

Plas thinks custom shampoos like those from Prose could grab up to 25 to 30 percent of the premium shampoo market over the next decade. Could an acquisition—by L'Oréal, no less—be in the cards?

He's not closed off to any ideas, but at this point, he sees two kinds of companies in the space. The first are innovators. The second are effectively financial companies that buy brands and try to take them to a global scale. While L'Oréal succeeded with this strategy with the likes of Kiehl's and Maybelline, he thinks they blew it with NYX by failing to respect the DNA of the brand. The worst outcome for Prose, he says, would be to sell to a large company that then destroyed the brand, perhaps even on purpose. After all, one of the tried-and-true ways that incumbents deal with competitive innovation is to buy it and kill it.

"You can't stop consumer expectations," says Plas. He's right. That train has left the station. Tomorrow's winners in consumer products are going to have to get on board, whether they want to or not.

Men Have Skin and Feelings Too

NICK ALLEN AND DAVE SKAFF, COFOUNDERS OF GEOLOGIE

Nick Allen and Dave Skaff have given men something they didn't even know they wanted—an enjoyable skincare regimen. In doing so, they are helping take the stigma out of men taking care of themselves. This is self-care for the frictionless era.

In Nick Allen's previous life, he cofounded two ridesharing companies. One of them was sold to General Motors, the other had to be shut down. While figuring out what to do next, he signed on with General Motors, helping the company work toward the commercialization of autonomous vehicles. On a fateful trip to Korea to assess GM's resources in the region, Allen decided to buy a gift for his girlfriend. Skincare is a big deal in Korea, and he decided to get her a bunch of products that she might not be able to find stateside. How could she not be thrilled?

She wasn't. It's not that she didn't appreciate the sentiment; rather, none of the products were . . . for her. "She thanked me and told me she loved me, but that the products weren't quite right for her," he says. "But I wasn't about to throw out four hundred dollars' worth of high-end

Korean skincare products, so I decided to try them myself." Up to that point, Allen was like a lot of men in that he'd never considered himself "a skincare person"—he rarely even washed his face in the shower. But he was instantly hooked. "This doesn't feel like a chore," he told himself. "In fact, I really enjoy it. I kind of feel like I'm pampering myself. My skin looks better. It feels better. Wait . . . why don't more guys do this?"

The next thing he knew, he was taking a bunch of fancy glass bottles with him on the kinds of adventures he and his male friends went on— backcountry skiing or motorcycling in the desert. At the end of the day, when everyone was sunburned or windburned, he'd pull the bottles out and say, "Hey, fellas, do you want to do a Korean facial?" At first, everyone laughed. The next thing he knew, he and five buddies were talking about the fact that while some of them had considered a skincare "regimen," none of them had ever known where to start.

The entrepreneur in him took over: he decided to research the current state of men's skincare. How does the average guy do that? While he did find a few brands, including Kiehl's and Clinique for Men, he also found himself confused. "They tell you to buy this one for oily skin and that one for dry skin," he says. "But I didn't know if I had dry skin or oily skin. By the time I got to 'combination skin,' I was dead in the water. I don't even know what that means." He ended up buying a bunch anyway, for research purposes. "But I didn't feel very confident in my buying decisions," he says. "It felt like a shotgun blast."

Next up: trips to the likes of Macy's and Neiman Marcus. Set aside the fact that finding men's skincare products presents a bit of a needle-in-a-haystack challenge in such establishments. It was the unfulfilling conversations that were worse. "I had some woman at a counter trying to sell me four-hundred-dollar-an-ounce La Mer," he says. "So I asked her why it was four hundred dollars. I did not receive a satisfactory response." So he walked down the street to Sephora, where he swears a woman in a headset was giving "a spin class for makeup." He left within about three minutes, worried he was going to have a panic attack.

"I'd tried to buy products in the three most obvious ways one might try to do so," he says. "And I failed. But it wasn't just that—I felt stupid, awkward, and kind of embarrassed. No wonder guys didn't want to do this."

And so he did what any good entrepreneur does: he decided to figure out how to do it right. "Guys don't know their skin type," he says. "They don't really know what to buy, and they don't want to go to the store. Our needs are pretty simple: we want a great product, we don't want to shop around for it, we want it to work, and we don't want to feel silly about it."

That's where Dr. Steve Xu comes in. Allen stumbled on Xu's name when he read an interesting paper on the efficacy of SPFs that the renowned dermatologist had written in 2016. He tracked down Xu's number and left him a fairly long voice mail. Two days later, Dr. Xu was on board. "He said, 'I love this. Guys come into my practice about a little mole on their arm and thirty seconds later, they're talking about skincare and Botox,'" says Allen, who jumped on the next plane to Chicago and signed him up. (Another Dr. Xu paper, from 2018: "The 'Dermatologist Recommended' Label: Is It Meaningful?" In this case, we're going to bet he says yes.)

Allen also reached out to an old friend, Dave Skaff. For the previous decade, Skaff had been running an e-commerce consulting agency in New York, where he'd seen firsthand the challenges of running direct-to-consumer health and beauty businesses. But he was ready for a change and the two dove right in—Allen took care of product and sourcing and supply chain, and Skaff took over the company's marketing efforts. (Full disclosure: Skaff is married to Duff's ex-wife. There may be no better example of a modern family than one in which the ex-husband buys his skincare products from the ex-wife's new husband.)

They raised a little money—just north of $500,000 from friends and family—and started out on a mission to simplify skincare for men without sacrificing quality in the process. New customers answer a diagnostic questionnaire to determine their skin "profile" and are offered a thirty-day trial set of all four of the company's products—a daily face wash, morning and night creams, and an eye cream—at a significant discount. When those samples run out, you have the option to sign up for a recurring subscription. At $148 every three months, it's not the cheapest stuff you can buy. But that's because it's also some of the best product on the market. More than 70 percent of those who order the trial set have converted to full subscriptions.

"There's a lot of crap out there," says Allen. "And that's because most brands treat men as an afterthought; they think we won't even know the difference." But it's not just that—50 percent of Geologie's customers (including one Duff McDonald) are newbies; they've never purchased these types of products in their lives. Most end up going through a very similar trajectory too: they start unsure about whether they'll be able to incorporate a skincare regimen into their daily routine, but before long, they're looking forward to it as much as any other part of their day. It's not a chore but a gift to oneself.

How do you make sure that customers stick around in subscription businesses, especially when it comes to something that they might run out of before the next shipment arrives? All without becoming the kind of subscription business that feels oppressive and/or unresponsive? You build functionality that allows ordering-by-text and early requests for refills. And you stay laser-focused on customer service. "Subscription is important to the business," says Skaff, "but it's more important for our customers that they're getting the right stuff when they need it. It's crucial that we're able to dial into the cadences that each person has and cater to them. The name of the game today is to be non-oppressive and totally focused on what the customer wants. So far, we've been able to achieve that."

When we ask about the *frictionless* concept, Allen points to various tools available to start-up founders that simply didn't exist when he was involved in his previous startups. "Starting a company is anything but frictionless," he says. "It takes a lot to get going. But we've come a long way in five years. The way it used to be, if you wanted to have functionality that enabled your customers who were excited about the brand to tell other people in an easy, seamless way, you had to custom-build it yourself. Today, there are probably ten or fifteen referral programs that are literally plug-and-play, and they only cost about twenty-five dollars a month."

For his part, Skaff worked with clients who spent *hundreds of thousands of dollars* to do just that, and usually without the desired effect. "There's a big ball and chain around the ankles of legacy brands that are tied to massive platforms that don't have any of those benefits," he says, "and they literally can't switch them off. The result is that they end up lumbering around when newer businesses like ours can start from the ground up and do so much more so much faster than they will ever be able to do."

Community is everything these days, and Allen and Skaff aren't missing out on establishing deeper connections with their customers. In early 2019, they began rolling out a series of social media posts that cover fifty or so topics, including basic skincare regimens, the ingredients in their products, and some good old-fashioned myth busting. "A lot of it is just the stuff that Dave and I have learned going through this process," says Allen. "There's a lot of BS out there. Take the new fad of using *charcoal* face wash. That's not good for your skin at all." Everyone hears, at one time or another, about some new product claiming "clean beauty" credentials through the use of "natural" products, but how much of that is science-based versus clever marketing that's capitalizing on insecurity? The guys at Geologie plan to be there to talk you through such things. Because who else is going to do it?

Allen recalls a meeting he attended in January 2019, during which someone pointed out that not a single man in the room had a clean-shaven face. So attitudes change. What's more, he adds, some things are more fun to do than others. "Shaving is something no one likes to do," he says. "It sucks. You're literally scraping your face off, and sometimes cutting it. But this is different. People *like* to pamper themselves. So your Dad didn't use eye cream? So what? A huge part of the message of our brand is that you don't have to be the man you thought someone else wanted you to be; you have the freedom to be yourself, including doing things that are healthy and good for you."

When Your Best Customers Are "Potheads"

ROBERT WANG, FOUNDER AND CEO OF INSTANT BRANDS

Robert Wang's Instant Pot took the friction out of meal preparation—throw your ingredients in, hit the button, and then come home to a nutritious meal. Then he used Amazon to blaze a frictionless trail to selling it to the masses.

Never heard of Robert Wang? Perhaps you've heard of his creation, the Instant Pot? One of the greatest success stories to ever come out of the "Fulfillment by Amazon" program—in which Amazon handles fulfillment of a seller's product in exchange for a cut—the Instant Pot might just be the perfect example of how technology has irrevocably changed the start-up game in the past decade. But let's not get ahead of ourselves. We should introduce you to Robert Wang first.

Wang is no newbie to the start-up world. The Shanghai-born entrepreneur, who slaved away in academia before joining Canadian telecom giant Nortel in 1995, has been around this block before.

In 1999, he joined a Nortel spinoff, Saraide, which was sold to InfoSpace for $365 million. But any hope of a retirement nest egg was destroyed when the tech bubble burst; Wang hadn't sold his shares of InfoSpace.

In 2000, he cofounded Taral Networks, a wireless messaging startup that later merged with another company to form Airwide Solutions. That's where Wang learned a valuable lesson: don't dilute your stake to the point of meaninglessness. He'd owned close to a third of the company out of the gate, but after raising some $45 million from outside investors, his holdings were down to just 1.6 percent. "That was a painful experience for me," he says. "We lost control in the first rounds. So when I started Instant Pot, I did it entirely out of my own personal savings. It's important to start without VC funding, because you keep total control."

The seeds of Instant Brands were planted in 2008, when Wang was kicked out of Airwide in a dispute over the company's direction. He knew it wasn't the right time to start another tech company. He also knew that he didn't want to start another one that sold business-to-business, or B2B. Even in an industry as large as telecom, the customer base had been too small and the purchasing cycles too long.

So what was the PhD in computer science with experience at three telecom companies to do? He decided to analyze some big trends and then put himself in the middle of them:

Trend 1: People don't have time.

Trend 2: People want to eat healthier. Research showed him that two-thirds of Americans are overweight according to body mass index calculations, and half of those people are obese.

Trend 3: People prefer being energy efficient and eco-friendly. In the United States, gasoline peaked at $4.11 a gallon in 2008. Electricity was high as well. Energy efficiency was in vogue.

"I designed the Instant Pot with those three trends in mind," he says. Consider the issue of time. The Instant Pot is *really* easy to use. Some of them don't even have a start button, and you can program them in ten seconds. You pretty much push one button, and off you go. It would be hard to save more time than that. The Instant Pot also cooks more quickly than conventional methods.

How did he know it was going to be successful? Well, he researched the Crock-Pot, which was introduced in the 1940s. When women started joining the workforce in sizable numbers, it took off, becoming a very popular appliance in the 1970s. By 2004, market penetration was already over 80 percent. But—and this is a *big* but—slow cookers were still selling 10 to 12 million units a year. "That's a pretty big market," he says, "and it was pretty clear that a device similar to the slow cooker—but better—would be in high demand."

Wang invested about $300,000 of his own money toward product development. It took eighteen months to get the product ready for market. Most Instant Pots have an assortment of buttons, but one thing Wang did was to make sure he nailed the comfort foods of most of the major ethnic groups who might want to use one: stew for Irish, rice for Asians, beans and chili for the Tex-Mex crowd.

The only problem is that he didn't really have any money for advertising. "My motto is to create value but stay frugal," he says. But not *that* frugal. Wang wasn't selling on Amazon at first, but in brick-and-mortar grocery and specialty stores. After a store owner in Montreal said he wanted to discuss the product, Wang jumped in his car and drove the two hours from Ottawa. After a lengthy conversation, the owner bit . . . and ordered *five*. "Five hours to sell five units," he laughs. "I realized that wasn't feasible, that there had to be a better way."

So he listed it on Amazon. He sold three units in the first week, without doing anything else. Within a month, people were writing reviews. The feedback proved extraordinary and was the source of many of the innovations the company has rolled out since. Wang had focused on building the best product and making sure they offered great customer service. And that's how the love affair with Amazon began. "It is the perfect marketplace for us because of our focus on product and customer service," he says. "People really read the reviews on Amazon as well as the ratings. When you get great reviews and ratings, sales go up. And when your sales crack the top one hundred, even more sales come in. And around it goes."

Before long, Amazon Wholesale approached Wang and asked him if he wanted to just go wholesale. The company already took 15 percent on Amazon Marketplace, and that still left Instant Brands on the hook for shipping and fulfillment. When he signed on for "Fulfillment by Amazon," it cut his shipping costs in half. He had to give some of that margin back when he took the final step to Amazon Wholesale, but volume increased by 50 percent. Recall that Wang is a computer scientist; he can do the math.

The Internet broke all the old business models. So what? We're now building them back up again. The Internet disrupted traditional jobs and employment and marketing, but we're seeing all sorts of new jobs, new kinds of employment, and new ways of marketing step into their place. Under "Fulfillment by Amazon," Instant Pots get shipped straight from the factory in China to Amazon's warehouses, and at one point, more than 90 percent of sales came through the site.[6]

In 2015, Wang started a Facebook group. "We're not selling mattresses," he says. "We're not a suitcase either. After people buy the Instant Pot, they still need recipes and want to share their experiences." At last count the group had more than 2 million members. In 2019, he agreed to a merger with Corelle, maker of Pyrex, and to stay on as chief innovation officer of the combined entity. And this time around, he'd kept control.

We've Got You Covered

JENNIFER FITZGERALD AND FRANÇOIS DE LAME,
COFOUNDERS OF POLICYGENIUS

Jennifer Fitzgerald and François de Lame took the friction out of a complex process—shopping for insurance. In doing so, they made it available to people who might not have even considered buying it. They used technology to allow human agency.

Why did the gold medalist win the race? Why did the winning company beat the competition? When writing history, one of the most difficult challenges is to avoid trafficking in a sense of inevitability. What do we mean by that? We mean that it's never easy to see into the future, and that things that seem obvious today probably didn't seem so obvious yesterday.

Throw in the X factors of luck and circumstance, and the idea of explaining why one company became the market leader while other companies languished can start to seem downright silly. In the majority of situations, what ended up happening wasn't what *was obviously going to happen*; it is simply *what did happen*. We are here because the route we took brought us to where we find ourselves today. We will be somewhere else tomorrow.

Sometimes, though, it's even more difficult to comprehend how we *didn't* see what was coming all along. Consider the case of Policygenius.

In 2012, Jennifer Fitzgerald and François de Lame were both consultants in the New York office of McKinsey & Company. Financial services companies, including insurance, love to hire consultants, and the two found themselves helping various financial institutions trying to solve the same set of questions. The first: Where was growth going to come from in an industry where revenues have been flattening over time? The second: What was the industry going to do about the fact that its main distribution channel—that is, the primary way it got products in the hands of consumers—was through brick-and-mortar real estate agents? The first question is one that every company eventually has to ask itself. The second was more existential: McKinsey had recently published a study showing that the average age of insurance agents in America was fifty-nine. In other words, the distribution channel was on the verge of retirement.

Neither consultant thought that the incumbent carriers were in much of a position to solve the problem themselves. De Lame, who had caught the start-up bug while in business school, thought that he and Fitzgerald should do it themselves. She wasn't so sure. "Early on, I was like, 'Meh . . . I'm probably twelve months away from making partner. I'm pretty cool where I am." But the start-up bug is more like a virus that doesn't go away, and de Lame eventually persuaded her to take a six-month leave of absence from McKinsey in 2013 to build a minimum viable product, or MVP, and see if they could make it work. The plan: they would build the Expedia of insurance products—what Expedia did for travel, Policygenius would do for "financial protection."

The plan was met with skepticism. A variety of efforts at "online lead generation" had already failed, and industry veterans kept repeating the same motto: "Insurance is sold, not bought." However, nothing speaks louder than numbers. Four years after launch, the company is one of the biggest players in interim life insurance and disability insurance. "For our life and disability carrier partners, we're probably their biggest source of growth," says Fitzgerald. "We're also a source of customers they weren't getting before, which is the under-fifty digital customer. Our average life insurance customer that we bring them is *ten years younger* than their other distribution partners were bringing." They've just launched home and auto insurance, both of which are taking off pretty quickly. Because of the success in other lines, it only took a couple of months for Policygenius to onboard the big auto and home carriers that they wanted on the platform. "They see us as a way to access a part of the market that they didn't know how to access before," says Fitzgerald, "which is exactly what we set out to do."

There's a wrinkle: while Policygenius has no plans to open its own brick-and-mortar locations any time soon, the surprise with this company is that it's not a purely digital operation. The first part of a Policygenius sale is typically digital—via the marketplace and the platform itself—but the next step is handled by an in-house team of actual people. And *that* is the part of the business that drives conversion and higher customer experience scores. These are intimidating purchases about which most people have low "category familiarity," meaning it's both important and high risk for the consumer. "When you need advice, the best model will be a blend of digital and human," says Fitzgerald. Won't it all go through AI, or artificial intelligence, eventually? Just ask Facebook, which was meant to be run by AI but is now adding more and more humans because their "self-learning" mechanisms failed spectacularly.

Is Polygenius worried about Amazon moving into their turf? They're *aware of the possibility*, although they don't seem too worried. After all, Google tried to sell auto insurance via Google Compare several years

ago, and failed. Whatever Amazon means to people—speed, convenience, and price—won't necessarily automatically translate into that
level of trust that the majority of people need if they're going to pull the
trigger on a decision as important as insurance. And then there's the fact
that digital commerce isn't always a no-humans proposition—sometimes
you still need an actual person involved. Take out a few people from
a process, and you can reduce friction. Take out *all the people*, and
you might not even be able to get the process started in the first place.
In that, Policygenius represents the third wave of e-commerce, the kind
where you still need an actual human to make the sale.

If it seems obvious in retrospect that automating insurance policy
price comparisons could be a viable business, it wasn't at the time.
They couldn't find any financial backers. Why? For starters, it was
early enough in the fintech revolution that attention hadn't yet shifted
to insurance. Those venture capitalists that *were* interested in fintech
were focused on lending, payments, and wealth management—more
than enough business models to disrupt before turning one's attention
to, YAWN, insurance. The second problem was that neither of the cofounders had a technical background—de rigueur for tech-driven startups—or, for that matter, any real management experience. (For more
on consultants and whether or not they can actually *run* companies, see
Duff's book *The Firm*, also from 2013.)

And so the cofounders were forced to rely on friends, family, and
colleagues, who contributed $735,000 to the cause. Nine months later,
in the summer of 2014, they launched the platform. It was never going
to be easy. For one, insurance isn't the easiest of products to sell. And
two, insurance companies themselves were skeptical about the wisdom
of relinquishing their direct hold on the end customer. Despite some
early and obvious traction, they still couldn't convince venture capital investors to step up, and were three weeks away from running out of cash

and not making payroll before they met the fund that led to their Series A investment of $5.3 million. From there, they were able to market a little more aggressively, and the Series B and C rounds of financing—$15 million and $30 million—were much more straightforward affairs. It's all obvious now. The herd has arrived.

How hard is running a startup? Say, if you're a McKinsey consultant whose been on the road five days a week and working ninety-hour weeks? "McKinsey was a cakewalk compared to the last five or six years," says Fitzgerald. "When prospective founders ask me advice saying, 'I want to start a company. It seems so glamorous,' I tell them, 'It absolutely isn't. It's like a punch in the face every day.'" Fitzgerald then admits what so many have suspected about not just management consulting but all of the MBA jobs that don't actually involve real operations: "The thing that people don't get is the challenge of building and retaining a team in a market like this, especially as you get bigger." Strategy? Check. Analyzing business models and figuring out pricing? Check. Competitive analysis? Check. "What's hard and unpredictable is people," she says. "And with two hundred fifty employees today, that's what takes up the lion's share of my time."

Of course, Policygenius still wants to hire smart people—"If you can get the best people working on a problem, you'll get to the right answer sooner rather than later," says Fitzgerald—but it also knows that it needs to find those who are less interested in compensation or an association with a big institution and more focused on getting lots of responsibility as well as steeper growth and career trajectories.

What will get in the way of continued growth? The first thing is that which has caused a few other online growth stories to stall: the rising cost of customer acquisition—fintech and specifically insurtech rank near the top of the list of the most expensive verticals in terms of price paid per customer. The second is good old-fashioned competition. When

Policygenius launched, it faced just a handful of competitors; today, it has hundreds. There's also a newsletter and a conference in Vegas. "A lot of competitors are coming in and trying to do exactly what we're doing," says Fitzgerald. "But that's fine, because having just done this, I know that strategy is easy and execution is hard. We've got a several-year advantage and a lot of deep and wide competitive moats."

They built one of those moats by following de Lame's instinct and focusing on content and search engine optimization in the first several years, on the assumption that they wouldn't be effective at acquiring customers through pure paid-advertising channels unless there was a really strong organic-driven base to it. "As you know, that's a long-term game," says Fitzgerald. "But it's tough to replicate, and it's the highest quality traffic that you get." The other thing they've done is built on their McKinsey experience of hypothesis-driven marketing. They're constantly trying new channels, figuring out what works, doing a surge of spending, analyzing the return on investment (ROI), and then figuring out if they need to spend more or less in that channel.

The next eighteen months, Fitzgerald thinks, will be the hardest part, given that they've chosen to essentially double the complexity of the business by adding a whole new vertical to it. "If we push through that," she says, "we're looking at a multibillion-dollar, household brand name. But there's a lot to do between now and then.

"Is this what this organization needs to look like when we are twice as big?" asks Fitzgerald. "I don't know the answer to that. It's just whatever you can make work. There is no right answer for organizational design." *That's the tough part, right?* we ask her. *The ambiguity?* "Yes, it can be pretty unsettling," she says. "You have to be fairly comfortable with ambiguity. That's a hard thing to articulate to people."

You've got that right, sister.

Schooled by the Machine

**MAX BENNETT, FAYEZ MOHAMOOD, AND MAHMOUD
ARRAM, COFOUNDERS OF BLUECORE**

The founders of data analytics company Bluecore have taken friction out
of the system for retail startups, helping them lure new customers in the
digital door and, once they are inside, helping them retain and nurture the
most lucrative among them.

When Max Bennett, Fayez Mohamood, and Mahmoud Arram founded
Bluecore in 2013, the plan was to build a solution that would allow retailers to more effectively collect and activate customer data—to trigger
communications in real time that would drive repeat purchases as well
as increases in customer lifetime value.

The idea was to make it easier for retailers to unify certain data sets
that would make such triggered email communication worthwhile. At
first, no one believed that they could offer a unified view of a retailer's
product catalog along with real-time analytics and activation. They
actually had to show the internal workings of the system to nontechnical
marketers to convince them that it was even possible.

The concept was also a new one, so Bluecore didn't have any actual
competitors per se. What they were competing against was habit and

history. Habit: retailers who sought to grow email revenue simply sent out more emails. History: a lot of retailers were used to trying to build their own email marketing solutions in-house. "There was no tool that did what we could," says Bennett. "We were competing against internal IT work or alternative methods for trying to grow email revenue that weren't personal."

Well, it turns out that it was possible—and profitable. Today, Bluecore's two hundred employees work with more than four hundred retailers—including Staples, Sephora, and CVS—to track and manage hundreds of product attributes to help determine what retailers should show shoppers next. Today, they house 500 million shopper email IDs and a cumulative product catalog that's second only to Amazon.

Email remains critical to customer retention, say the founders, because of a few factors:

1. You've already identified that person as a customer.
2. Microsoft, Google, and Apple have helped with intelligent filtering and categorization, so those emails that get through to most of us tend to be read.
3. When retailers use automation technologies that employ triggers, predictive audiences, or personalization, they can drive email ROI to levels that are two to five times higher than social media or search.

"We're trying to help retailers push the retention line further and further to the left so that they don't have to keep throwing money at Facebook and Google, which are essentially the new malls," says Mohamood.

The software integrates with retailers' live product sets, which gives them visibility and insight not just into those items that shoppers have purchased or put into their shopping cart, but also every product a shopper has ever viewed, clicked, searched, or browsed while on their site.

Most of us have received emails about "abandoned" carts. It turns out those are quite effective. But the Bluecore team takes emailing to a whole new level, telling customers things like "a product you were looking at that was out of stock is now back in stock" or "a product that you were interested in has just decreased in price."

Bluecore's AI-driven decision engine determines the timing and content for the next best communication based on insight into individual shoppers' onsite behaviors and how specific product-shifts influence their actions. All of this drives relevance for shoppers and increased revenue with less effort for brands.

The statistics are clear and simple, to boot:

- Messages that feature merchandise placed in shopping carts and then abandoned generate sales 2 percent of the time. That's four times the rate of the next best options—price decrease notifications and dynamic emails featuring items that were viewed but not placed in carts.
- Customers who receive emails that showcase products they have window-shopped or placed in shopping carts are most likely to open these messages. Open rates for both types of efforts top 40 percent.
- When customers are made aware of price decreases on products they've displayed interest in, more than one in ten, or 10 percent, click through to a brand's website.

How does a company prioritize which message they should send to their customers? To solve that question, Bluecore has developed an AI-driven "reinforcement learning model" that figures out the right mix—per customer, per campaign type, per product, per offer—without anyone doing any work. "All they have to do is push a button," says Bennett, "and they're automatically generating new revenue simply by virtue of using machine learning to prioritize their messaging."

The more data a machine-learning model has, the better its performance can get. In many cases, though—image recognition and natural language processing come to mind—there can be a long initial period during which the machine-learning model underperforms the status quo. The good news for marketers is that machine learning can trump the status quo—sending the same message to everyone—quite quickly.

Why? "Because we enable you to go from one email for everyone to automatic generation of segments to one-to-one communication," says Bennett. "And there's no period of underperformance because the status quo in marketing is so weak." Bluecore's machine-learning applications do more than just provide insight to their customers about their own customers; they go one step further and auto-optimize and auto-learn. Most of us have been offered the chance to "subscribe" to one product or another from the likes of Amazon—pet food, toilet paper, etc. And most of us have chafed at the idea of subscribing to such things, because we don't want to be locked in to purchasing on a schedule that doesn't necessarily line up with our own usage. People are tired of being sold subscriptions.

Bluecore helps retailers solve that conundrum by using machine learning to help its customers figure out the least annoying time for you to get the message that you might want to consider replenishing your stock of whatever item you might need once again. Call it a "nonsubscription subscription," or telemarketing minus the friction. Either way, it's the future.

Chapter 5

FRICTIONLESS COMPETITION

Fifty years ago, Bob Dylan sang "Love Is Just a Four-Letter Word." As the founder and CEO of a consumer products company, I can tell you that the four-letter word in 2020 has nine letters in it: *inventory*. In my world, there aren't many *dirtier* words than that.

I didn't always know that. But my experience at DwellStudio taught it to me in a pretty punishing way. Ask anyone who has sold an actual product: from an operating perspective, you are only as flexible as your inventory allows you to be. More to the point, when you carry inventory, you are placing big bets every single time you place an order. Some items, or SKUs, will sell at high volume. Everybody loves it when that happens. But other SKUs won't. What makes it difficult is that you have to place your bets *before* you know which is which. At DwellStudio, we had some SKUs that sold so well we literally could not keep them in stock. Solving that problem isn't as easy as it might seem either. Why not just order more of them? Well, we would when we could, but we were also cash-constrained by other SKUs that didn't sell as well, with the result that we were rarely able to buy enough inventory of the top sellers to capture all the demand upside. It's one of the most frustrating parts of the business.

When you're dealing with imported product, too, the lead times are so long that even when you *know* something is a huge seller, it can still take ninety days to get re-upped on it. Sales cycles are so short today that in ninety days, you'll probably have lost the interest of the customer who wanted it so badly just three months earlier.

There's also the fact that if things start going *really* wrong, inventory can literally break you. After the financial crisis, DwellStudio had lumpy cash flow—so did everybody—and our inventory became a significant drag on the business. It's one of the reasons I ultimately sold the company.

On the flip side, the less inventory you carry, the more flexible you can be. Taken to its extreme, zero inventory equals infinite flexibility. I saw that at Wayfair, a company that offers some 13 million SKUs but holds almost nothing in inventory. How do they do that? That brings us to the concept of drop-shipping, the idea that you can carry wholesale products on your site and sell them without ever touching them. That's one of the central secrets to Wayfair's success. Amazon's too. They are marketplaces that sell other people's products.

My aha moment happened when I realized that I could combine parts of DwellStudio and marketplaces like Wayfair or Amazon. I used to think that you *couldn't* build a branded consumer business without inventory. But Amazon showed me that wasn't true, that you *could* build a branded consumer business without inventory.

That's when the lights started to go on—the moment my nascent plans to start another business came into clearer view.

There's an old saying in showbiz: "Never follow a banjo act

with a banjo act." So I never once considered competing with Wayfair or Amazon head-on. They're too good at what they do.

Wayfair showed me that you could be a consumer business without owning any inventory if you could position yourself as the "pass-through." The only question is whether you can add value in that role. Amazon and Wayfair both do it via price, selection, and service. The opportunity, at least for me, was in design.

The question I kept asking myself: How could I use technology to create a nimble company that was adding value but wasn't actually *touching* anything? That didn't *own* anything? (In other words: How could I make it more *frictionless?*)

The challenge, as I saw it, was to bring to bear the same level of design I had at DwellStudio, but to somehow do everything else Amazon's way—in other words, to create a high-quality design brand that didn't take on inventory risk.

Inventory? What's that? In the old model, you had to try your best to predict demand and then order your batch. And no matter how good your crystal ball, you were always over or under at the end of the day.

I'd tried to figure it out gradually, but then it hit me all at once: the toolbox was sitting right in front of me. I just needed a killer tech team to make it happen.

I envisioned running an entire operation in a virtual world:

- A world in which we could introduce new products *every single day*, see what customers liked, and then start tailoring the product line for them.
- A world in which we didn't need to make anything *until we'd already sold it*, where things that didn't sell didn't cost *anything* except the time spent designing them.
- We'd aim wide, not high, at the very same addressable markets that Wayfair was, with similar price points.

- By making furniture on demand, with drop-shipping, we would slash the delivery window for custom-made furnishings from months to weeks.

That's an offering, I concluded, that did not exist. Why? As far as I could tell, no one had thought of it. And even if anybody had, they would have rightly concluded that it was impossible; marrying good design and low prices is a tall order. I knew I'd have to strip out some major costs along the way to make it work, but I was undeterred.

Let me make one thing clear too: I love design. Rather, I love *good* design. I have zero interest in peddling crap to the masses. That's not interesting to me. I also refuse to sell someone an inexpensive dresser that comes in four hundred pieces that they have to put together themselves. The only way to make *that* cheaply enough is to use scrap wood. That's not me.

So I decided that I was going to throw everything I knew about the design business out the window and retool it for the Internet era.

Home furnishings is a massive and growing market—$102 billion in annual sales in the United States alone. That's a big enough market to feed several unicorns. But it is also a market in need of reimagining. The moat around The Inside derives from superior design. We use custom proprietary design for both frames and fabric. We use virtual manufacturing to provide an endless number of proprietary SKUs. An accessible price point means customers can change their spaces—and their furniture—more often, making their decor decisions less stressful. The Inside gives shoppers a curated experience, with on-demand product, making the purchase experience both more gratifying and more fun.

We also completely reimagined the supply chain. I don't

think I'd even heard of the term "supply chain efficiency" before Wayfair, but these days, it's one of my favorite things. Supplier scores? That wasn't part of my vocabulary either. But both are a big part of the future of retail, two of the levers you must pull in order to conjure up the Holy Trinity of fast, cheap, and good.

Every day, I spend time thinking of where we can squeeze a little more margin out of those parts of the business that the consumer never even sees. At The Inside, we've made design part of the supply chain, with an in-house design studio able to create and execute exclusive designs. Once a customer places an order, the furniture is made on demand, a capital-efficient approach to a traditionally capital-intensive category. Made in America, our production is both environmentally conscious and sustainable. It takes us under three weeks to make the furniture, and cost-effective shipping adds just another week or so, making the whole process something under four weeks.

To repeat: we have exclusive designer patterns and capsule collections on affordably priced furniture that arrives, direct-to-consumer, in under four weeks via UPS. Remember when you had to wait fourteen weeks to get a couch delivered? We deliver in less than *thirty days.*

We don't make anything until we've sold it. Nothing at all. And here's the thing about that: it turns out that making "nothing" is very cost-efficient, and we've passed those savings onto the consumer. The only reason I can sell you a $399 queen-size headboard is because I have stripped out all of those costs. Call it Furniture 2.0. Or Home Furnishings 2.0. The point is that it's not what we used to do; it's what's next.

While at Wayfair, I came to understand the fundamental genius of that company's business model, which is to be a marketplace that carries no inventory. There have always been marketplaces, that's true. And eBay proved how compelling it

could be to be a marketplace online. But it's still pretty revolutionary for a branded company that *sells you products of its own
design.*

Today, with Google Analytics, we can see where customers
hover longest on our website. And we optimize, by way of A/B
testing, all day long. What else do we do all day? We talk, constantly, about the central issues driving any online retail outfit:
design, marketing, and our website.

And then we give the customers what they want. Our marketing is in a constant state of iteration. When Britt and I saw that
Andrew Dudum built Hims partly on the back of advertising in
actual locker rooms and on bathroom walls, we began asking
ourselves, "What is our locker room? What is our wall?"

What's all that supposed to add up to? The same thing that
you've heard about any number of breakout business success stories these days—we remain in the midst of one of the greatest
reshufflings of corporate and economic power in the history of
corporations and economies themselves.

Every new generation rejects something that its predecessors
had once deemed worthy; it's an essential part of growing up
and establishing one's own identity. At the same time, some
ideas, technologies, and brands have shown an ability to stand
the test of time, to *endure*. In time, they become . . . *incumbents.*

Why do incumbents endure? In many cases, it's because they
are the most compelling of the alternatives, for reasons of cost,
quality, convenience, or all three. But in many others, it's because of effective marketing, and the creation of brand images
that successfully obscure the fact that competing products or services are cheaper (cost), better (quality), or more readily available
(convenience). The most successful brands can demand a premium in the marketplace, for the simple reason that consumers

place a value on reliability—the feeling that established brands are less likely than the alternatives to somehow disappoint. (See McKinsey & Company, Colgate toothpaste.)

When barriers to entry are high, too, brands inevitably begin extracting a premium from their customers whether they deserve it or not. The worst of this scenario is when there's an effective monopoly. (See Blockbuster video.) But as the case of Blockbuster shows, nothing lasts forever, especially when you don't treat your customers the way they should be treated. The single most important reason that Netflix survived its first few years wasn't because of what it did (DVDs by mail), but what it didn't do (charge extortionate late fees). It's much different today, but Netflix got its start as an antiproduct—"Anything but Blockbuster."

Why do you—why does anyone—switch brands? Because you've changed your opinion, based on what you perceive to be new information. A lot of the time, though, you can't be bothered to look for new information about a specific product or service, because it's not worth it to you to do so. (Or at least that's how you perceive things to be.)

Duff shaved with Gillette razor blades until he stopped shaving entirely. Why? Was it because he thought Gillette razor blades were perfect? No, it was because he couldn't be bothered to spend the time gathering the information his rational mind would require in order to make a change. And because Gillette razor blades can be bought everywhere. And because no one had bothered to convince him that there was a better way, a better brand. Duff wasn't alone. Gillette has long owned the vast majority of the razor blade market.

But that was before the Internet made it easy to do research before buying, to investigate new brands and their cost-quality-convenience trade-off, and to find out what other people think about them. In those days, brand recall was one of the most important things a company could rely on. And the big just got bigger.

Those days are gone.

Combine the two factors above—every new generation's desire to reject the choices of its forbears *and* the ability to compare alternatives at a cost approaching zero—and you have a recipe for revolution. Brand power isn't what it used to be. Information is the great leveler. Market share still matters, but not nearly as much as it used to.

Customers will always want lower cost, better quality, or greater convenience. That hasn't changed. But because they can now find one or more of those things much easier than they ever could before, loyalty just isn't what it used to be.

Consumers want a five-star experience at a three-star price, whether that's in travel, health care, or health insurance. And they believe they are entitled to it. If you build a business operating under that premise, you have two very important ingredients for success, and it doesn't matter who you're competing against. Nobody gives a shit about Procter & Gamble anymore. Before he stopped shaving entirely, Duff bought a new razor and blades from Harry's.

We don't all land on the same spot on the cost-quality spectrum. Some people will pay more for better quality, some people want to pay less and only care if the thing works. The two things we all want are convenience and ease, and the Internet offers both up in bounteous supply.

Who wants to walk into a mattress store? Who wants to spend their time there? Nobody. It's all about consumer experience. We want to do away with friction. Today, everyone wants what they want in a box at their front door, and that includes mattresses. Casper isn't a wildly successful startup because they sell the world's greatest mattresses. It's because of their marketing.

The Internet has also facilitated the rise of something totally new, or at least the perception thereof: personalization. Prose blends hair products specifically tailored to their customers' hair. Stitch Fix looks in your closet, and sends you clothes that don't just fit your body—they also fit the idea of who you think you are. Here's what customers are saying: "Sell me something for me! Don't just serve me up *anything*!" And that extends all the way into careers: "Don't tell me what job I want! I'm going to make my own!"

What does it all mean? It means this: *Operating in the shadow of an incumbent is no longer a silly idea. It is THE idea.* It's quite clear that millennials don't have long-term customer loyalty: How else to explain the rapid shifts from Myspace to Facebook to Instagram to Snapchat? This is especially pronounced in financial technology, where incumbents realized that they should outsource much of the development of fintech to startups after trying it on their own. According to PwC, the percentage of financial institutions planning to increase their fintech partnerships over the next two to five years currently sits at 82 percent.[1]

Consider insurance companies. Do millennials know any of the names their parents did, such as Prudential? Duff switched his homeowners' insurance to peer-to-peer provider Lemonade, based on the quality of their app. His life insurance might soon follow: Seattle-based Tomorrow sells life insurance and offers estate-planning services through an app. Founder and CEO Dave Hanley told Bloomberg in mid-2017 that it was the easiest capital raise he'd ever done. "I actually never got on an airplane to raise any of this money," he said. "Investors came to us."[2] We spoke to Dave, and report back on the conversation on page 000.

"Digital rewards first movers and some superfast followers," says a recent McKinsey report. "In the past, when companies witnessed rising levels of uncertainty and volatility in their industry, a perfectly rational strategic response was to observe for a little while, letting others incur the costs of experimentation and then moving as the dust settled. Such an approach represented a bet on the company's ability to 'outexecute' competitors. In digital scrums, though, it is first movers and *very* fast followers that gain a huge advantage over their competitors. We found that the three-year revenue growth (of over 12 percent) for the fleetest was nearly twice that of companies playing it safe with average reactions to digital competition."[3]

Millennials simply do not have the loyalty framework that previous generations had for big marketing-spend brands. Nor, for that matter, do their parents. Duff has made a hardcover photo album of his daughter's year at Xmas for the past five years, starting when she was four. If this were twenty-five years ago, Duff probably wouldn't have entrusted this task to anyone other than an established photography brand such as Kodak. When I asked him whether he used Snapfish or Shutterfly to produce the book, his response was, "To tell you the truth, I don't know." Why? Because he doesn't care. He's actually used both, with the decision of which to go with based on who was offering the better deal the moment he was ready to order the new books. (Usually around December 20. And they have always arrived in time for Xmas. We do live in amazing times.) In 2012, by the way, Kodak's own effort in the space, Kodak Gallery, which it had bought not built (originally Ofoto, launched in 1999), shut down, and Shutterfly purchased the assets out of bankruptcy. Type KodakGallery.com into your browser today, and you will end up on Shutterfly's site. Talk about disrupting the incumbents—this fish swallowed the whale. (There's also the issue of *trust*: millennials and Gen Z do not trust big brands, which lack a level of transparency that they now expect.)

Here's the good news: *If you fail to topple an incumbent, you can always sell to them.* They may be so slow moving that you can build a business with the explicit intention of selling to them. Marc Lore did it *twice*—in 2011, he sold Quidsi (parent of Diapers.com and Soap.com) to Amazon for $545 million; and then in 2016, he sold Jet.com to Walmart for $3.3 billion and joined the Arkansas behemoth as part of the deal. We all know that the e-commerce landscape is being dominated by Amazon, which accounted for 4 percent of retail sales in the United States in 2017. Walmart wants to get to a place where they are at least players. What might be next? They could acquire Wayfair. Lore has had some out-of-the-gate success at Walmart, with acquisitions such as men's clothier Bonobos helping drive online sales growth of 60 percent. But in recent quarters, the retail giant has stumbled against Amazon, and Lore is in the hot seat.[4]

On-demand hiring platform TaskRabbit was founded to offer frustrated consumers help with life's most challenging tasks, like standing in line at the Apple store or putting together IKEA furniture. IKEA bought the company,[5] its brand, and its digital expertise in September 2017.

There's a third way, too, after beating them or selling to them. It's working with them. Collaborations can add new value and cache to old brands, and many old brands are working with new entrepreneurs to try to do just that. (Call them sub-entrepreneurs.) What do these new strategic relationships look like? Everything from helping a company manage its supply chain to coming up with new marketing ideas.

Consider that old warhorse Gillette. The company offers personalized grooming advice for men on its website using its latest iOS app. Customers take a picture and try different looks. They can also connect with grooming experts and third-party non-competitive producers of grooming products. Men feel they are receiving the personalized experience they demand while the platform participants benefit by interacting with a large pool of potential buyers.[6] The retailer Target has partnered with IDEO and MIT Media Lab to study food trends. In September 2017,[7] L'Oréal hatched a social media ad campaign called the Founders Series that highlighted recent brand acquisitions and their entrepreneurial roots. Why? According to the *Wall Street Journal*, in a recent survey by public relations agency Edelman, 50 percent of respondents felt that "successful entrepreneurs" were credible company spokespeople versus 20 percent who felt that way about celebrities.

A fourth way is to join an innovation ecosystem. The most recent example of how living in someone else's ecosystem can be a road to vast wealth is that of Apple, the iPhone, and apps. But there are many more, including the connected home and retail/communications partnerships for mobile commerce. A recent example: with the announcement by Amazon, JPMorgan Chase, and Berkshire Hathaway that they will be getting into the health insurance business by providing it to their own employees, you can be sure there's a gold rush in the offing for startups in that space, either to sell or to collaborate.

The following profiles showcase some of the most exciting entrepreneurs wielding the power of *frictionlessness* to disrupt incumbents today. They're not the ones you've probably already heard of, like Warby Parker or Casper. They're the ones that most people haven't heard of yet.

But they're not just people who decided to take on the incumbents. They're people who figured out how to take the *friction* out of old ways of doing things in order to improve their competitive edge. Because it's true: while it's never been easier to start a business, it's also never been harder to acquire loyal customers and build long-term value as a result.

Advances in technology have eliminated a lot of the friction for *anyone* who wants to start a business and compete. You don't need a lawyer or some fancy consultant to set yourself up with a website and social media assets these days. All you've got to do is turn on your computer, tap a few keystrokes, and you're good to go.

And there's more. As entrepreneur Polly Rodriguez wrote on TheHelm.co, a website devoted to companies founded by women, "The B2B start-up marketplace has gotten unbelievably efficient at solving every potential pain point founders face. Payment processors, HR software, customer acquisition channels, office space, and cleaning crews all have their own mini-markets for consumer-facing startups to choose from."[8]

Five years ago, most people wouldn't have heard of the concept of performance marketing, also known as growth marketing. The term refers to the science of gaming paid-marketing channels like Facebook, Google, and Instagram for big returns and low customer acquisition costs. It's fascinating stuff, and also *required* if you're going to compete in today's digital landscape. Luckily, more and more performance marketers are being groomed every day. At The Inside, we've taken the money we no longer need for capital expenditures and poured it into human capital and performance marketing.

Don't get me wrong: you can't just decide to start a business— any business—and think that you can cobble together a bunch of bespoke tools and be good to go. You still need to *own* something that's yours, the thing that distinguishes you from what's already out there—your competitive advantage. The centerpiece of any competitive advantage is *a thoroughly unique idea*. In days of yore, the successful companies were the ones that took an idea and layered talent, connections, and drive on top of it. In today's digital era, you can add the ability to generate traffic and gather and analyze data to the pile.

But let me stress the importance of the *idea* again. Because if you don't have that *something* that's yours, you run the risk of doing things for the wrong reasons and making all sorts of questionable decisions to convince other people that you do. The Theranos scandal is exhibit A of the above phenomenon. Originally lauded for its claim to have discovered a revolutionary way to test blood—capable of running dozens of tests on just a single drop of blood—it quickly devolved into a sordid story of scientific and financial fraud.

If you ask me, the Elizabeth Holmes story is the most striking cautionary tale of a founder ever told. She never had a real product. But she was dressing like Steve Jobs and flying around the country in a corporate jet. I saw her during her heyday, at *Glamour* magazine's Women of the Year awards in 2015—she was an honoree that evening. Not three weeks later, the *Wall Street Journal* revealed Theranos as a sham. What motivated her? I can't say for sure, but it seems likely that money was a major factor. And money isn't on the list of good reasons to start a company. If there's no *there* there, it's never going to end well.

If there is a *there* there, on the other hand, it's hard to think of a better time than today to marshal your resources and put together a team to go out and get it. In the pages ahead, you will be treated to the stories of a number of entrepreneurs who took a great idea and ran with it. Sorry, are *running* with it.

Everybody Wins, Including Your Dog

BRETT PODOLSKY AND JONATHAN REGEV,
COFOUNDERS OF THE FARMER'S DOG

Brett Podolsky and Jonathan Regev took a complex scenario and made it frictionless. The Farmer's Dog allows you to feed people's best friend fresh and healthy meals every day—without the hassle of making those meals yourself.

Why do consumer goods cost what they do? In the years before the Internet, that was usually a straightforward question. The manufacturer would figure out how much it cost them to make, say, a can of dog food, and then tack on a margin when selling that dog food to a wholesaler. That wholesaler would then turn around and figure out how much it cost them to distribute to the huge grocery stores, pet retailers such as Petco, or smaller pet stores, and then tack on a margin themselves. And then retailers did the same. By the time you were at the cash register, the "cost" of the dog food had been marked up three times. As a consumer, your job was to decide if price-versus-quality made sense to you.

One of the most thrilling things about the direct-to-consumer revolution is how the most forward-thinking companies have turned that whole pricing structure inside out. Somebody's still got to make the thing, so there's usually still going to be a manufacturer's markup. Today's direct-to-consumer retailers then buy it (at wholesale prices), tack on their own margin, and sell it to you. But instead of simply pocketing what would have been the retail margin for themselves, this new breed of companies has taken those margins and divvied them up in a new configuration between themselves, the product, and their customers. There are three possible outcomes:

- **Better Price**: You get the same thing, just much cheaper. Think Warby Parker or Casper mattresses. Both companies took friction-filled categories with absurdly high margins and delivered a ton of value and convenience to the end consumer.
- **Better Quality**: You pay a little more, but you get *a lot more* for that extra expense than the premium over retail would suggest. Brooklinen is a great example of that. Their sheets aren't cheap, but they're cheaper than great sheets *used to cost*, and great quality. They layer on the frictionless convenience, and the analog options look much less interesting.
- **Better Quality and Price**: You pay more or less the same amount you would at retail, but for a much better product. That's our model at The Inside—we take some of the savings from eliminating various costs in the supply chain and put them toward being able to offer our customers price-versus-quality options that aren't available at retail.

Which of the above three describes The Farmer's Dog, which delivers fresh-made dog food on a subscription program? It's scenario number two, in which dog owners may pay a little more to feed their pets on a per-day basis, but in doing so are able to provide a quality of food—freshly made, no preservatives—that is simply not available through traditional retail channels. It's not cheap to make fresh dog food, but the trick is that they start by adding the cost of doing so onto the price wholesalers pay, not the one retailers do. You may pay a little more, but you're getting a lot more for your money. Everybody wins, including your dog.

Like so many of the companies we interviewed for this book, the origin story for The Farmer's Dog is shockingly straightforward:

Someone had a problem.

They couldn't find a solution among available alternatives.

So they solved it themselves.

At some point, they realized that they couldn't possibly be the only ones who've encountered that problem.

They started a company to find out if they were right.

They were.

In this case, Brett Podolsky's dog Jada had stomach problems that just wouldn't go away. No branded pet food seemed to work. Different vets offered different advice, but one common denominator bubbled up: feed her a homemade meal of chicken and rice. "I started wondering why vets didn't just recommend home cooking as an everyday thing," he says. "But it's because it's pretty hard to give dogs all the vitamins and minerals they need when you do." At the same time, Podolsky's research on Jada's behalf had also convinced him that commercial dog food is too highly processed. "Think of it like serving junk food to your kids every day of their lives," he says. "It's okay now and again, but if that's the only thing they eat, they're eventually going to have health problems."

How did cofounder Jonathan Regev get involved? It started when he was in between apartments and sleeping on Podolsky's couch. "I thought he was insane," says Regev. "My dogs ate dog food, like everybody else's—but Jada went through a health transformation when he started cooking for her. It was the first time I'd ever realized that dogs eat *food*."

One revelation was followed by others: Why is dog food so processed? Because it needs to be "shelf-stable" so that it doesn't go bad before you buy it. How could they design a business model around delivering fresh food for dogs? One way would be to use a subscription model—unlike humans, dogs eat a remarkably consistent amount from one day to the next. If you ranked subscription programs by thoroughness and timing of consumption, dog food would be a contender for number one. The fresh-versus-processed food choice had already moved front and center regarding human food, and Podolsky and Regev figured the cultural timing was right. But just as nobody feeds themselves a filet mignon every night, there is surely a limit to how much they will spend to feed their dogs. The trick was to figure out if they could do it for an amount that made sense to everyone involved.

That's where technology came in. Dogs come in many shapes and sizes. There are two-pound dogs that eat half a pound of food a week, and hundred-pound dogs that eat that three times a day. And some people have more than one dog. Throw in all the variables—breed, age, appetite, activity levels, food sensitivities—and the cofounders realized that they needed to build a custom platform to service all those subscriptions.

Purina never had to do that. Neither did Blue Buffalo. The brand names in dog food have built billion-dollar businesses using wholesale distribution, which means that they only have a few hundred or thousand customers to deal with. Direct-to-consumer companies interact with *every single one* of their end customers, and in the case of The

Farmer's Dog, those customers all want different amounts, and on a different cadence. The only way it would work was if they could . . . *take the friction out of the system.* They had to know how much to send you and when to send it while also keeping open the ability to modify subscriptions on the fly.

In the end, they realized that they would be spending more on food and more on technology than the incumbents. What could they spend less on? Marketing. "Dog people are quite special," says Regev, "in that you don't just love your dog, you love *all* dogs. The hope was that once people realized what we were doing, then they would tell all their friends." The promise was that if it worked—and it seems to be working quite well—the incumbents wouldn't be able to compete with them head-to-head.

Why?

One: It's hard to sell fresh food via wholesale.

Two: By selling wholesale, the giant pet food brands have forsaken a relationship with their end customer. That's where data comes in. If you have no understanding of what your end customer *really* thinks, it's hard to be responsive, let alone innovate on their behalf.

The flip side is that Podolsky and Regev needed to solve the problem of how to scale the business from a people perspective. Customers who have questions about their dog's diet aren't going to want to talk to a bot. "The fantasy would be to have them come to the website, sign up, and live happily ever after," says Regev. "But that's not realistic. Customers need to know that we're real people that care about their dogs—because we do." But it gets complicated: the frequency with which people reach out tends to be high in the beginning and less so along the way. How do you staff that kind of customer service? In late 2018, that meant moving to a new office in Williamsburg, Brooklyn, because they had so many people working the phones.

Another complication: they needed to find food processing facilities that use the raw ingredients of human food, not dog food. And the problem with *that* is that those facilities are naturally nervous about being associated with dog food. ("That tastes like *dog food!*") It took a while to find someone willing to do so. For a year and a half, Podolsky and Regev rented a kitchen in Brooklyn and made all the food themselves. They managed, but it was hard work.

Have no doubt, the competition is coming. In 2019, Petco and partner JustFoodForDogs opened a kitchen in New York where they intend to make two thousand pounds of fresh food every day. And sales of fresh pet food in grocery and pet stores jumped 70 percent between 2015 and 2018, to more than $546 million. That doesn't include online sales.[9]

When it came to the question of financing, neither founder wanted to raise outside investment—they'd bootstrapped with a $5,000 investment apiece and pay that was well below minimum wage. But two things happened. First, they realized that they couldn't physically cook for much more than one hundred dogs. And second, they met Eurie Kim, a venture capital investor who understood their mission of upending an entire industry without sacrificing the thing that brought it all about in the first place. A $2 million seed raise followed, then an $8 million A-round and then a $39 million B-round.

"We started this company being customer-centric in the sense that we were trying to solve a real problem," says Regev. "We built a platform to handle individual needs, and hopefully, we can add things like treats and supplements." Duff risks their scorn and asks them whether they plan to make cat food, because he and his girlfriend Joey have three of them. Alas, there are no plans to do so as of yet. At that point, the two dog-owning cofounders look at him with sympathy in their eyes—not because they don't make cat food, but because he doesn't own a dog.

The Four Seasons of Coworking

RYAN SIMONETTI, COFOUNDER AND CEO OF CONVENE

Ryan Simonetti's Convene takes the friction out of renting office space—for both tenants and landlords. Tenants who want more than a cookie-cutter WeWork space get all the amenities. But Convene's real value proposition is for landlords, who use Convene's technology to wring more money out of every square foot they own.

Convene describes itself as the leading provider of premium meeting, workplace, and hospitality-driven amenities to institutional landlords and their enterprise tenants. That's a mouthful, I know. Just think of it this way: the company works with landlords to overhaul and redesign tired office space, and then provides ongoing services, including food and beverage, concierge, catering, meeting and event hosting, flexible workspaces, wellness, and a range of technology services delivered through a proprietary technology platform.

That sounds like WeWork, right? But there are big differences between the two. Just as OpenTable would tell you that the restaurateur is their primary customer, and Airbnb would tell you that the homeowner is their primary stakeholder, Convene views *the building owner* as their primary relationship. WeWork, on the other hand, considers its primary relationship to be with the tenants. If that isn't clear enough, Simonetti offers a different analogy: "We're Equinox to the competition's Planet Fitness." Lastly, only one of the two companies has seen its public reputation ravaged in the past year, and it's not Convene.

More than half of Convene's revenue comes from mature companies with $1 billion or more in revenues. That's a different business model than WeWork, which leans more toward freelancers and small enterprises. What gets Simonetti most excited is the company's technology platform, Elevate. The goal is to help both landlords and tenants simplify their lives; tenants should soon, he says, be able to book a meeting room, order food, or add guests to a building's security with a single app.[10]

Convene comes from a hospitality heritage. These days, Simonetti says, it's more of a "coworking" business. *Was that a pivot?* we ask "It's not a revolution, but an evolution," he responds. "Look, every founder or entrepreneur will tell you that you're pivoting nonstop."

The $260 million that Convene has raised to date is not a small number, but it pales in comparison to the many billions that WeWork has raised from a combination of debt and equity investors, Softbank in particular. Why the differential? "We're partners, not competitive threats, to building owners," says Simonetti. "Specifically, to the largest property owners in the United States. When we grow our business, we don't have to raise billions, because our landlords are putting up the money. Collectively, they have way more money than we do, and way more money than Softbank does. We're really using *their* balance sheets to scale our platform." (Again: only one of these two companies seems to have raised *way too much money* than it could responsibly handle in the past few years, and it was not Convene.)

Convene, like WeWork (or even Uber) is, at its root, an excess capacity play. They are using technology to help old-school landlords stay abreast of the times by offering their tenants a frictionless experience. Technology also allows Convene to do it at scale: think of the modularity of it all; the same design team can roll out fifty different office designs without a whole lot of extra trouble.

But it was Simonetti's back-of-the-envelope math—his TAM calculation—that really blew me away. TAM stands for total addressable market—it's what you, as an entrepreneur, are chasing.

Believe it or not, during the entire time I built and ran DwellStudio, I never once had the concept of TAM explained to me. The mistake I'd made at DwellStudio was that I'd been aiming too high. Given our price points, DwellStudio's TAM was just the 4 million or so homes at the top end of the interior design market. That market, I should add, is jam-packed with competition. Wayfair's TAM, on the other hand, was the 230 million or so households in the mass-market middle.

To say the point hit me like a lightning bolt would be an understatement. I suddenly understood that I'd been going at this all backward— I'd started with designing what I thought were great products, and our pricing and TAM kind of fell out of how much it cost us to make them. Wayfair came at it from the other direction: they sold products that they could price at a level to reach the largest possible number of consumers.

I'm not a dummy; of course I knew that at DwellStudio I'd been aiming for a more affluent customer than Wayfair's. But I'd had no idea about the difference between our respective TAMs. When you're in the trenches every day, it's difficult to synthesize that kind of information. And because I hadn't started DwellStudio the way Niraj Shah and Steve Conine had started Wayfair, I never really did.

When DwellStudio was at its peak, we enjoyed tens of millions in annual sales selling at "masstige" prices in Target. To what had I attributed that success? Design, of course. But I suddenly realized that the primary reason we'd done such huge business with Target was because there was a massive addressable market that had been underserved. But not that massive: Wayfair also helped me understand that DwellStudio really had nowhere left to go unless we went for mass.

That insight informed my vision for The Inside. My hunch was that you could do both: you could be laser-focused and customer-centric while also emphasizing good design. I just had to figure out how.

This was the TAM calculation we landed on with The Inside: Our average customer sits in the $75,000 to $100,000 income range, which is 14.4 million addressable homes. Add to that the people who make up to $200,000 and you have 43.3 million households, which is just under half the country's total.

Before we return to Simonetti, I should point out that if you want to build a venture-scale business, your TAM better be gigantic. You better know what it is, and you better have a price point that fits right into it. And here's the thing about that: if you're looking for a huge TAM, you are generally talking about mass-market products. That's Wayfair's whole play. But Simonetti and Convene have managed to surface a gigantic TAM in the context of class A office space—that's premium product. And that means we're talking about *serious* money.

So let's get to that TAM:

- There are 400 million square feet of office space in New York City, of which 50 percent or so is class A. Call it 200 million square feet.
- Industry research shows that over the next decade, somewhere between 10 to 30 percent of that space is going to be consumed in the "convenience" format, not the legacy format. So that's

somewhere between 20 to 60 million square feet moving into this category.

- If Convene snags a 10 percent market share, which isn't crazy, given the company's already strong brand, that's anywhere from 2 to 6 million square feet of office space that could move onto Convene's platform.
- Convene has shown the ability to monetize office space at between $150 and $200 per square foot. That's $300 million to $1.2 billion in revenues.
- With 40 percent unit economic margins, the numbers start to get really large, really quickly.

Not only that, if Simonetti's global ambitions are anywhere close to achievable, it gets even nuttier. If Convene secured even a 1 percent market share of what stands to be hundreds of millions if not billions of square feet of repurposed office space, you're talking about a valuation worth many, many billions. Convene is WeWork without all the bad news and the ridiculous leverage, and with a ton of superior design. Let's see where this goes . . .

Start Your Startup Here

EMILY HEYWARD, COFOUNDER OF RED ANTLER

Emily Heyward's Red Antler takes the friction out of the entire go-to-market process for startups. If you've got a great idea, Red Antler can help you brand it, plan it, and launch it.

This sounds a little obvious, but it's not: startups that don't launch with a pretty clear idea of who they are—and/or are also able to convey that image to customers—will get lost in the noise.

It wasn't that long ago that you'd lose the debate with a venture capitalist over whether it was worth spending money on branding before you'd totally figured out product-market fit. But VCs have come around too.

At The Inside, a branding studio called Partners & Spade helped us with our branding and copy, our voice, and our tone.

One of the most important things I've learned at The Inside is that you've got to stay focused on what the consumer thinks about, even if you yourself are fascinated by something else. I love rethinking my supply chain; I do it every day. And in the early days, we told our customers a lot about those aspects of the business—about how we were cutting costs, and where—and it turned out that the consumer didn't really care. It wasn't what was drawing them to the brand.

If you ask me, too, I think the much heralded "move fast and break stuff" strategy of Facebook lore is a little overrated. I think you should get it right before you start pushing it out. I don't mean that you shouldn't pivot or iterate along the way—that's a daily task—but you shouldn't launch something if you know it isn't working.

My own investors pushed me to launch in just under four months in mid-2017. But we were building some very sophisticated technology, including 3-D rendering and proprietary customization tools that really weren't ready for prime time. Not only that, the dominant e-commerce platform, Shopify, wasn't really capable of handling the 11,000 or so variants we had. We tried a million different hacks to make the business work on their platform, but we just couldn't do it in the end. We had to trash the whole thing and build our own platform a year later. It was a hard lesson to learn.

I'll never know, but I bet if we had been working with Emily Heyward, we could have avoided a lot of that pain. She and her team at Red Antler have seen it all before. Red Antler and a few others, that is. In the world of cutting-edge branding, there are three agencies that seem to matter: Partners & Spade, Pattern Brands, and Red Antler.

When I think of Red Antler, I think of a company that has a few tricks up its sleeve. When it vets potential clients, it looks for companies that can strip out costs and deliver more to the consumer, often due to supply-chain disruption. Heyward and cofounder JB Osborne also have an ability to partner with brands with powerful stories to tell—names like Warby Parker and Casper.

Both had worked in the advertising industry out of college, and while they'd enjoyed it at first, they both eventually started to feel like they were focused on the wrong problems. They spent most of their time trying to come up with new and exciting things to say about old and broken stuff.

At the same time, they realized that no one was really talking about brand building as part of the entrepreneurial journey. People were focused on product, and design was being discussed in the context of user experience, but there wasn't really an embedded understanding of what it meant to build a brand. They saw an opportunity to create a branding company focused on startups, and that's what they did, launching Red Antler in 2007. They worked alongside founders like Susan Feldman and Ali Pincus of One Kings Lane in their early years.

"Our thesis was that startups that think about brand from day one will have a competitive advantage," says Heyward. "It was an uphill battle in the beginning, but everyone has come around in the past decade. Startups are launching with a much more polished and robust image than they were before."

Red Antler works with its clients on everything a business needs to launch—strategy, packaging design, branding, advertising. That includes everything from name and brand identity to a website that tells their story effectively while also being easy to use. And Red Antler throws as many resources at them as necessary—the company once had eighteen people working alongside *just two* cofounders at one of its clients.

Heyward says that the most significant change she's seen in the past decade is how much more quickly—and with much more precision—companies are able to find their audience. "When I'm scrolling through Instagram, I'm constantly coming across these tiny fashion brands with incredible photography that clearly know my exact taste and what I've bought and the sites I've visited," she says. "You can identify these incredibly small slivers of the population and reach them with the absolutely perfect message. It's pretty hard to tell the difference as you scroll through your feed between those new fashion brands you've never heard of and an ad from Cynthia Rowley."

She acknowledges that many niche brands will die off due to being starved of repeat business from their customers. But she does think that it's possible to launch a brand with focus and then expand from there— consider Warby Parker, which started with just a few styles and an at-home try-on offer and today oversees an eyeglass empire.

Red Antler has worked with Casper (mattresses), helping five founders land on a unified mission. They've also worked with Burrow (furniture) and Goby (toothbrushes). Duff loves Goby—his daughter, Marguerite, loves it even more, and starts her nightly brushing session by saying, "It's GOBY time!" What do all those companies share? Each of them feels like they have a genuine reason for being, rather than the result of a couple of MBAs wanting to start a business, looking through various industry categories, and seeing where they might gain a foothold.

In most cases, too, the innovation wasn't just in the product but in the supply chain as well—and by disrupting the supply chain, they were able to reduce cost while maintaining quality.

But the final layer was that they are able to tell a story on top of that—one that delighted people. "Casper is an amazing example of that," she says. "Before Casper came around, nobody could tell you the name of their mattress brand. Not only that, people thought they were crazy to try to sell mattresses online. But the founders knew that brand identity was going to be the difference.

"And then from there comes the hard work," she continues. "Brand building doesn't happen overnight. You can't skimp on it or say you're only going to spend ten grand on it. You've got to spend time. You have to really think about your target audience and the story you want to tell them, and what's going to resonate. You've got to build in lots of layers that are going to continue to surprise people and delight them at every turn. You have to be funny and magical and unlike everything else."

Heyward thinks the most exciting action in years to come is going to be when heretofore digitally native brands move more aggressively into physical retail, the way that Warby Parker and Casper have done. "How do you create a truly omni-channel experience?" she asks. "I don't know that anyone has really solved that. To do so, they're going to have to use customer data in a way that doesn't freak the shit out of them."

Disrupting Insurance the Artist's Way

DAVE HANLEY, FOUNDER AND CEO OF TOMORROW

Dave Hanley's Tomorrow takes the friction out of two of life's most depressing administrative tasks—buying life insurance and making a will. In doing so, they've allowed people who wouldn't have ever considered estate planning to assert power over their financial futures. The insurance costs money, but the will is free.

Many of the most successful people among us follow a two-part pattern in their lives. They spend the first part focused on their own needs. And they spend the second on the needs of others less fortunate. Dave Hanley started on the second part first: in the 1990s, he worked at Grameen Bank, the pioneer of microfinance founded by Muhammad Yunus. (Yunus won the Nobel Peace Prize as a result.) A letter of recommendation from Yunus helped Hanley get into the Stanford Graduate School of Business. (The head of admissions told him, "You're going to want to keep this letter.")

After graduating in 2003, his passion for music combined with a career at RealNetworks, where he ran product for the Rhapsody music service, among other things.

By 2007, though, he was looking for a new opportunity. He found it in Shelfari, an online book club that had just five thousand users at the time. The company convinced Hanley to join as vice president in charge of marketing. Sixteen months later, they had 2 million users, and Amazon swooped in and bought it.

How'd they do it? Hanley employed the lessons of "virality" he'd heard in a lecture given by Reid Hoffman, one of the founders of LinkedIn, the gist of which was: in the frictionless online world, the way to grow is to turn your own users into a professional promotion machine. The trick that worked for Shelfari was an email that asked, "Do we read the same books?" Those emails lured new readers to Shelfari, which sent out new emails, and so on.

Hanley cofounded Banyan Branch, a social media consulting agency, in 2009 because he thought he would be able to use the monies it generated to fund another start-up idea. But the funding vehicle turned into a success in its own right, with early clients including the Bill & Melinda Gates Foundation, Fox, Disney, Porsche, and Intel.

What do you do when the company you started to fund a passion project starts to look like a long-term success itself? In Hanley's case, he and his partner decided to build it to a size at which they could sell it. "When we were a thirty-person company, we were able to write each other $300,000 checks at the end of the year," he says. "It was nice. And while we enjoyed the work, we decided to build a growth company and sell it." Deloitte Digital stepped up to the plate and bought Banyan in 2013. Hanley stayed on for almost three years.

That's when a good friend told him that he'd been "asleep" since the sale to Deloitte, having settled into a nice job with a compelling salary. She sent him a few books to help him wake up, one of which was *The*

Artist's Way, by Julia Cameron. In doing the daily exercises that the book suggests, Hanley came up with six company ideas in a little more than two months.

The idea for Tomorrow—partially derived from his experience at Banyan—was one of those six. As more of the agency's young employees got married and began having children, Hanley discovered that few had life insurance and almost none of them had wills. One of the reasons, as anyone who has or hasn't bought life insurance or written a will knows, is that the process is daunting and expensive. So Hanley set out to make it easy—to make it more *frictionless*.

LegalZoom and other providers charge hundreds of dollars to create a will. But the marginal cost of delivery of a will in template form—this is something done by software—was zero. Hanley predicted a race to the bottom and figured out that Tomorrow would enter the space by making it *free*. (There is nothing as frictionless as *free*, people.)

Here's where the virality principle kicks in again. Tomorrow was going to acquire customers by offering them something for free. And consider what a will contains: a list of loved ones, including one's spouse, children, guardians, executors, and the like. The viral aspect of the project should be landing like an anvil on your head: when people ask other people to be the guardian of their children in the event of their passing, the people they've asked are now tuned into the idea of getting a free will from Tomorrow. And that's when you sell them life insurance. The company has partnerships with ten different carriers, including AIG and Aflac, and makes money whenever any of those companies makes a sale to a Tomorrow customer.

There are other ways to sell life insurance. You could start an online agency, like Jennifer Fitzgerald and François de Lame did at Policygenius. But at some point, says Hanley, in any industry where players compete head-to-head in digital marketing, all potential margin will be transferred to Facebook or Google. Or you could build a new market offering them free products, and then bring your customer base into insurance without having to compete head-to-head in the first place. "We're going to build a series of free or inexpensive products adjacent to financial services and then bring our customers to the financial products we know they need but were just too busy to buy in the first place," he says.

As it was with Shelfari, Tomorrow's customers are also its best salespeople, at least as far as new users of the free estate-planning product goes. "Those social features drive somewhere between a third and a half of our new users," says Hanley. What else is he planning? "I'm not going to share that with you," he says. "I have a bunch of ideas, including some you'd think were super wacky, but they're all quite relevant to what we're doing."

Of course, it's never easy to make something easier. Each of the fifty states has its own estate laws regarding trusts and wills, its own insurance licensing procedures, and its own requirements for such important issues as power of attorney. By the time we spoke to Hanley in late 2018, Tomorrow had accumulated 205 licenses to sell just two products—wills and life insurance.

What convinced venture capitalists to fund the company to the tune of some $7.5 million to date? Two things: The first was the combined track record of Hanley and his cofounders, which included four exits. The second was that the insurance industry was poised for disruption.

Life insurance is a multitrillion-dollar industry but the largest player, MetLife, has just a 4 percent market share. That's called fragmentation. Not only that, the median age of a life insurance agent is nearly sixty years old, which means there are fewer and fewer salespeople in a position to sell to young people.

In just 120 days of operation, Tomorrow slashed its customer acquisition costs to just 10 percent of their original levels using digital and television advertising. They've got board members with relevant experience, including one who made the seed investment in Credit Karma.

We ask Hanley about Amazon, which has been making noises about entering the insurance space itself, quite likely as an insurance agency itself. "I don't know what they're going to do," he says, "but here's what we will do: we will try to make sure we're not going head-to-head with them. We will continue to acquire customers through our free products, not through insurance. Because, as everyone knows, when Amazon breaks into new businesses it plays the long game, and that can be painful for startups trying to compete with them."

Allow us to translate that for you: Amazon is well known for gaining market share in new realms by using its financial wherewithal to underwrite predatory pricing—they absorb their own losses while undercutting rivals to such an extent that they force them into submission. See the sordid saga of Diapers.com for more.

That friend who told Hanley to wake up? Her name is Georgie Benardete, and she's Hanley's girlfriend now. The awakening brought him back to where he'd started, with an eye to working on things that could produce maximum impact for humanity. And also somewhere else. After too many roles where he's tried to do everything, at Tomorrow he's narrowed his responsibilities down to just a few: raising capital, recruiting, and strategy. "I have to make sure I'm not a robot," he says. "I have given myself the gift of setting up the culture of a company that allows the CEO to be absent on any given day." That's the kind of gift that keeps on giving.

Decadent and Healthy

JUSTIN WOOLVERTON, FOUNDER OF HALO TOP CREAMERY

Most ice cream companies hide their calorie count in the small print. Justin Woolverton's Halo Top took a different route: They put it right there, in large print, on the front of the pint. In doing so, they took away decision friction and put the pint in the hands of happy customers.

Just like David Greenberg of Updater, Justin Woolverton began his career by taking the safe (if still challenging) route of becoming a corporate lawyer. But Greenberg had found a measure of career satisfaction as a lawyer before heading out on his own to start Updater. Woolverton had no such luck. Four years into his law career at white-shoe firm Latham & Watkins, he realized that he'd made a huge mistake.

Just like medicine or finance, the legal profession tends to beat up on its new recruits, handing them all the grunt work in exchange for the promise of a better tomorrow, when, as a senior lawyer, one is able to push all the grunt work onto the latest young lawyers. "You think you can see a light at the end of the tunnel," he says, "when things will get better." But sometimes they don't.

His breaking point came on a case that should have made him

happy. He got to fly to Hong Kong. He got to stay in a nice hotel. He found himself in front of a tribunal. "It was all the stuff you dream about," he says, "and then I realized that I still wasn't having a good time—that if this was the light at the end of the tunnel, I shouldn't have been in the tunnel in the first place."

How did he decide to start an ice cream company? Did he do a TAM analysis? Did he sense a chance to go direct to consumer? Was he going to leverage efficiencies from the cloud? Nope. None of that. He decided the old-fashioned way: "I'd made that ice cream for myself and I loved it," he says. "And I'm not that weird of a guy . . . I'm pretty much middle-of-the-road . . . so it just hit me that if I liked it so much, then there must be a market for it." In other words, he realized he was average, and it was the secret to his success.

Put another way, he went with his gut. "I didn't do some sort of MBA SWOT analysis or anything." (SWOT, a core of most entrepreneurship courses, stands for Strengths, Weaknesses, Opportunities, Threats.) Once he realized that the idea could be real, he did what any intelligent person does and researched how to make ice cream on the Internet. Did you know that there are some universities in Canada that offer ice cream science as a major? Well, Woolverton didn't either, until he did, at which point he downloaded and absorbed all the free course materials they have online. A year or so of trial and error with a local ice cream maker followed, and then it was go-time.

"For me, that was the really appealing part," he says. "I don't know about you guys, but I really enjoy figuring out how something works—even an entire industry." That's one of the signs of the true entrepreneur: a desire to first figure it out and then figure out how to do it better. It's a personality trait.

And so he dug in. First, he learned how to make ice cream. "That's really fun," he says, "and I don't mean that sarcastically." Then, how to start a business. ("Also fun, also not sarcastically.") And so on: how a P&L works, how to go to market in the consumer-packaged goods industry, pricing, margins, distribution.

The result: Halo Top, a pint of ice cream with just 300 calories, 20 grams of sugar, and 20 grams of protein. And flavors like Red Velvet and Pancakes and Waffles. It used to be that going low-calorie meant giving up an enjoyable experience. As one writer wrote, "Halo Top delivered on the promise that it was possible to somehow be both decadent *and* healthy."[11]

Woolverton never once considered raising venture capital. Instead, he spent about $150,000 of his own savings. That got him through the R & D phase and another year thereafter. At that point, he and Doug Bouton, his cofounder and another refugee from big law, raised $300,000 from family and friends, which gave them another two years. And then another $700,000, also from family and friends. "I say I regret going to law school and becoming a lawyer," he says, "but it did have its benefits—one of which was learning how you can found a company and still end up losing control of it." Woolverton gave up some equity, but retained 100 percent voting control at Halo Top.

Halo Top isn't for everybody. But the product has been good since the beginning. Despite that, they almost went under several times. Ask any entrepreneur: that's not your worst-case scenario. It's your always-case scenario. But they managed to stay the course until . . . things went bonkers. In a good way.

What happened?

First, they changed the packaging to make it clearer what Halo Top was—a low-calorie ice cream that still tasted good. They put the number of calories on the *front* of the container, in big numbers. "When you're competing on the store shelf, that's your billboard," he says. "With that change, we were able to say what we were—and how we were different—from all the other nameless ice creams."

Second, they made some improvements to the science behind the ice cream to make it more resilient through the supply chain, so that it wouldn't deteriorate in any way before it got to the end customer, the consumer.

Third, a bomb—the good kind—landed in their lap. A writer for *GQ* magazine decided to try and eat nothing but Halo Top for ten days straight. "We had no idea it was coming, and when it landed in my Google news alert, I could barely bring myself to read it," says Woolverton. "He tried to eat *nothing but Halo Top* for ten days straight? But it was an honest and funny and ultimately flattering article. After that, the thing just utterly exploded."

And by that, he means, for a brief moment, Halo Top was the best-selling ice cream in the country, ahead of both Ben & Jerry's and Häagen-Dazs. Armed with the knowledge that they were consuming far less calories than from the two name brands, consumers started buying two, three, or four pints of Halo Top at a time. That was unprecedented, at least for . . . your average person.

The *GQ* article hit in January 2016. By the end of the month, they'd sold more than in all of 2015. In February, sales doubled from January. In March, they doubled again. They haven't looked back. From just $230,000 in sales in 2013, the company topped $100 *million* in 2017. By late 2018, they'd gone international, and it was following the same kind of trajectory as had happened in the United States.

Next up: opening a handful of company stores around the country, expanding even more internationally, and adding new flavors—Peanut Butter Cup and Birthday Cake the most recent entries among them.

About 150 people worked at Halo Top just before press time, when it was announced that Wells Enterprises, the second-largest ice cream manufacturer in the United States, had purchased the brand. Woolverton did not stay with the company, meaning that his foray into ice cream is done for now. The big question is why he even went on in the first place.

Ice cream hardly seems like the kind of industry that would benefit from the Internet, but it's just like everything else in that regard. "It sounds almost corny to say it, but without the Internet, without the social media networks, I doubt that a new company could challenge incumbents like we did," says Woolverton. "You just have that built-in magnifying glass to where if somebody likes something they can tell four thousand people at once versus just talking to a couple of friends."

If he'd tried to launch in 1980, he continues, the best he could have done in terms of advertising would have been newspaper ads (expensive), billboards (expensive and inefficient), and maybe food magazines. Today, Halo Top can target online ads using psychographics, geographics, and demographics. "It's absolutely crucial to making our limited marketing dollars work," he says. "If we didn't have that, I doubt Halo Top would be able to exist."

Or consider this: because Halo Top is more or less Greek yogurt in ice cream form—all natural to boot—the company tracked down people who liked, say, Chobani enough to post about it, sent them a coupon for a free pint, and let social media do its magic. "That's not quite organic growth because we had to give away free pints," says Woolverton. "But the ROI was great. And it's a lot more organic than a paid Facebook ad." But they buy those too. And Instagram ads. And Twitter ads. But they're all targeted to people who are more or less likely to at least consider trying a pint of Halo Top. Where there was once friction in a marketing budget, there is now precision.

Social can cut both ways, though. Halo Top has been dragged

across the social media coals not once but twice—it was accused of understating calorie counts and of underfilling its pints. When we asked Woolverton about that, he said he couldn't comment, because of ongoing litigation, but he did tell us something else. "This job is already way too stressful. To be sitting there trying to cheat people at the same time? I wouldn't be able to handle that kind of stress myself."

Not only that, it grated that someone was *suing* the man who brought us Halo Top when what we really should have been doing was give him awards.

Woolverton came, he saw, and he conquered territory in ice cream that no one knew existed. We'd bet a pint of Birthday Cake that he'll be back soon enough, that the party isn't over yet.

How to Ace "the Walgreens Test"

ANDREW DUDUM, FOUNDER AND CEO OF HIMS

Hair loss and erectile dysfunction are such friction-filled subjects that men will literally ignore them until they're a real problem. A startup named Hims removes that friction and more, including trips to the doctor and the pharmacy as well.

Andrew Dudum has been around the start-up block. He sold his first company to Telefónica in 2012. He founded a venture fund, Atomic, in 2013. He sold another company to Snap a few years later. The man solves problems for breakfast.

The idea for Hims, he says, derived from his experience watching dozens of friends struggling with a couple of signature issues—erectile dysfunction and male pattern baldness—but everyone was struggling alone; no one really wants to talk about such things. The stigmas around them are real, and the conversation, for what it is, is a stunted one. What if, he thought, there was a place for a personal wellness brand for men that tackled the stigma head on, simultaneously eliminated the need for one of life's great hassles—the nonemergency doctor's appointment—and threw cheap pricing and stylish packaging into the bargain to boot?

"There was a massive education and conversation gap," he says, "so we launched with a primary mission of educating and normalizing the topics men were worried about, then getting them the most authoritative information, signed off by phenomenal doctors." What's more, he was going to deliver it at affordable prices of twenty to thirty dollars a month versus historical prices that reached into the hundreds—and with convenience.

And let's be serious about this: no one wants to talk about erectile dysfunction. Dudum is quite confident that most of Hims's customers don't have a doctor they feel comfortable calling about *anything*, let alone the intermittent failure of one's "manhood."

"If we can make people more comfortable about seeking treatment, they can have a positive experience with the health-care system, which is typically a pretty terrible system to interact with," he says.

When Dudum launched Hims, the statistics suggested that 50 to 70 million men in the United States suffered from hair loss, but just 100,000 of them were using medication to combat it. There are a lot of reasons that might be the case, including ego, but it turns out that one of the most important is that it was just too much of a pain in the ass—it wasn't that they weren't able to look themselves in the eye and acknowledge that they needed it, they just didn't have the time or inclination to look *someone else* in the eye and do the same. Remove the *friction*, in other words, and you've got a gigantic customer base just waiting to sign on.

What's fascinating about Hims, though, isn't those things that it shares with other direct-to-consumer brands, including affordability, nice packaging, and education. It's what's happening behind the scenes: as of late 2018, the company had stitched together a network of some one thousand physicians across all fifty states that were writing more pre-scriptions, combined, for the above issues than any other medical in-stitution out there. (See? Size *does* matter.) And Hims's trick is that the customer interaction is less like a traditional doctor's visit than it is like buying something off Amazon. For 80 percent of Hims's customers, it all happens on the phone—medical consultations, treatment plans, and prescriptions—and in thirty minutes or less. The days of going to the doctor for that little blue pill are over.

In other words, Hims's isn't just selling you medicine under a spiffy new brand name. It is also combining D-to-C pharmacy with a D-to-C health provider network with D-to-C insurance coverage to get you what you want. But the brand still matters. "Our long-term vision is to be a brand that people love and trust to help them take care of some really serious stuff," he says, "whether that's hair loss, sexually transmitted diseases, high cholesterol, or smoking cessation."

That's why you don't just see Hims marketing in your Facebook feed. The company's subway ads are well known in New York City, in part because of the controversy that the city created by accepting ads for erectile dysfunction while rejecting things for, say, female sexual health. For Hims, the reason to be on the subway is that it gives a potential cus-tomer thirty seconds to a few minutes or more to consider a relationship centered around something as sensitive as erectile dysfunction. That's why Hims also advertises on porn sites (home to 75 percent of the time men spend on the Internet, most of it by themselves) and urinals, where you are highly incentivized to look straight ahead without turning your head even a few degrees to one side or the other. In all of the above situations, the potential customer has the time to actually digest the marketing message.

(It's kind of terrifying if you think too much about erectile dysfunc-tion drugs advertising on porn websites. One of the obvious reasons that many men can't sustain erections in real-life situations anymore is because they've been desensitized by all the pornography out there.)

Dudum has also stressed the idea of "creating inventory" rather than buying it. Example: while Hims can and does bid for ad space on open marketplaces like Facebook, they also do things like suggesting that the 24 Hour Fitness chain might be interested in selling space in all of its locker rooms around the country. The chain got paid for an asset that had hitherto lain dormant, and Hims has created an exclusive and long-term inventory that will last for years. According to Dudum, up to 50 percent of the company's marketing spend is targeted at such initiatives.

Dudum's ambition has been helped by the fact that a number of major drugs have gone off patent in recent years, including sildenafil, the main ingredient in Viagra. But if you thought Pfizer—the maker of Viagra—would come after Hims on its own turf, selling Viagra for two dollars a pill, you thought wrong. What they've done is launch a contradiction in terms—Viagra Generic—for thirty-five dollars a pill. The way things used to work with expired patents, customers could either continue buying the brand-name drug at top dollar or the generic version for cheap. But you can add two more options to that list: a half-price "generic" version sold by the maker of the original brand (Viagra Generic) or a truly generic version that's now associated with a different kind of brand (Hims). But that's really just three categories in the end: branded, generic, or a branded generic. Hims sells you the third.

So how do you keep customers on a subscription? In the case of Hims, that's easier than, say, a meal-delivery service. Because you need to keep using Hims products for them to be effective. And while a few competitors have sprung up—Roman (www.getroman.com) is going straight at Hims (www.forhims.com)—the behind-the-scenes complexity of what Hims is doing with doctors and pharmacies and insurance carriers is a barrier to entry to all but the most ambitious competition.

It's also a barrier to exit for his customers. Dudum is friends with a number of entrepreneurs who have built successful direct-to-consumer operations, including Harry's and Warby Parker. While he wishes them all the best, to Dudum, the main issue regarding long-term competitiveness is whether or not a company's product passes what he calls "the Walgreens Test."

Simply put, if you've signed on to buy something via subscription, and the shipment has a glitch—whether that's a delivery fail or if you happen to be out of town at the moment you need what you need—can you simply go get a temporary replacement at Walgreens? You may like your Harry's razor, but you *can* buy a replacement down the street. What can't you just zip out and replace? Things that come via prescription, such as erectile dysfunction or male pattern baldness medications.

"The product works not just because they're great medicines," says Dudum, "but because the friction of getting them from someone else is very high. You simply can't walk into Walgreens and walk out with a substitute product unless you're prepared to pay an insurance co-pay, go to your doctor, talk to the nurse, and then wait in line at the pharmacy." Is he worried about the likes of Roman? Not really. With some estimates forecasting up to 90 percent of what we do in the doctor's office literally moving online in the next five years or so, Dudum thinks there's going to be plenty of business to go around.

But the fight for market share is now, and for that reason Dudum says Hims focuses on hiring experienced, battle-tested execs instead of the young and impressionable, while also keeping head count as low as possible in order to keep decision-making out of the clutches of bureaucracy. The entire team is just forty-five people, versus the four hundred or five hundred you might have found at a company with similar revenues in a different historical moment. "I want the most senior people trying to solve the big problems in the business, not helping people get ramped up to do their job," he says. "But the opportunity is so big that everybody is just rolling up their sleeves and building things." That's the kind of thing you need to do when you take something like the healthcare system, gut it, and then build it all up again under a new name.

Chapter 6

FRICTIONLESS ORGANIZATIONS

Offices are not what they used to be, but the changes are more than just the ones you've read about—remote workspaces, shared cubicles, WeWork, and the like.

At DwellStudio, we had a traditional turn-of-the-millennium office. We employed fifty-five people, including a design team of seven—meaning overhead of at least $500,000 in design salary, not including benefits. We had landlines, even fax machines. At The Inside, I employ just one designer in New York and seven others remotely.

One of the first questions I asked myself when scoping out just what the offices of The Inside should be was: *Should we even have telephones?* Answer: No. And there are no fax machines either. (A millennial wouldn't know how to work one anyway.)

When I think of the money we used to spend on IT infrastructure, I can't believe how much has changed. We had a server room at DwellStudio, for God's sake. Today, everything we do is in the cloud, and our corporate operating expenses have plummeted. (Thanks, Jeff Bezos!) You can outsource almost anything these days except for your core competency.

It cost me $140,000 to build the first website for DwellStudio, and the hosting and development fees on e-commerce platform Magento were thousands of dollars a month. (If that doesn't shock you, consider this: Goldman Sachs spent more than $1 billion to build a consumer-facing website that they then shut down.) Not only that, once they had you, they *had* you. If we needed some new functionality from our site or a fix, we pretty much paid Magento whatever they asked. Why? Because they held our digital fate in their hands. Today, Shopify costs seventy-nine dollars a month, and while it's not quite enough for our needs at The Inside, it's more powerful than anything I could get my hands on in 2012.

There's been a seismic shift in the workforce too. Even employees want to be entrepreneurs; they want to be freelance. They might work at a company, but they don't want to work at it in a traditional way. Nobody wants to sit in a traditional office anymore. They might do coding for you, but they're going out surfing afterward.

As for regular work hours, ye olde nine-to-five? Those are so yesterday. One of our early hires, who has unfortunately since left us, was Ivy Zhang, whom I poached from Amazon. Jeff Bezos has clearly figured out better than anyone how to build an organization for this kind of business, and I wanted someone who could tell us some of their secrets. Ivy worked in the Home category at Amazon, and when she was with us, we picked her brain every day about how they did it at Amazon, especially when it came to customer experience. With Ivy, I knew I was getting a Jeff Bezos protégé; what I didn't know was that Ivy would show me the new standard for remote work. Instead of being in the office, she showed me it was possible to get her work done from somewhere like the South of France. Ivy has as strong a work ethic as I've ever seen, it's just that her ethic doesn't include the structural and geographical rigidity of yesteryear. Ivy left us for greener pastures in the summer of 2019, when she decided to start a restaurant in New York City. I can't wait to eat there. The woman knows how to serve customers, I can tell you that. And if she's as good at the food part as she is at everything she taught us, we are all in for some delicious meals.

On that same note, let's be clear about something: the patriarchal system of past offices is a thing of the past. You can't operate that way anymore. It matters for people looking for jobs, but also for those running companies.

My venture capitalists were pushing me to build a team at The Inside from the start. But there's only value in a team if you can retain that team. Half of these people don't want to be hired. I'll take them any way I can get them if the productivity is there. Keep in mind, too, that the flip side of hiring is firing. I had a really big staff at DwellStudio. When 2008 happened, I didn't get rid of any, to the detriment of the company. So today, I'm hesitant to hire people anyway. I want to be able to grow and shrink at will. Freelancers have little to no onboarding process. And let's just be honest here: when things get tough, it's easier to let someone go whom you haven't seen every day for the past five years. That may sound ruthless, but it's also true.

It used to be that job seekers had to find a company that did a thing, and then go where that company wanted you to go. Today, it's *you* that gets to choose the thing—and if you put in the hard work and develop the insight and responsiveness to stay competitive, it's more likely than not that the company is going to come after you, not the other way around. They used to pay people big bucks to relocate. Today, relocation is practically off the table, and the big bucks go to the top talent, wherever it chooses to be.

Ninety-five percent of people believe they need new skills to stay relevant at work.[1] But only a third of millennials feel their organization is making the most of their skills and experience, and 66 percent expect to leave their employer in less than five years.

But the smartest among us are figuring out how to work better with others. Because there's no solo effort anymore; it's all about constant collaboration, team building, and working smarter together. They used to ask if you knew how to use Word or Excel when you applied for a new job. These days, you better know how to use Google Hangouts and Slack. There's a reason Slack was able to raise $250 million in 2017 from Softbank and other investors, a raise that valued the company at $5 billion. By becoming the de facto online platform for team communication, the company has burrowed deeper and deeper into the enterprise, the very game strategy that brought us enduring successes like Microsoft and Oracle. But it's also positioned itself at the center of the collaborative process, and collaboration is the future of work. Ask a millennial if you don't believe me.

So let's get into this section by asking what I consider to be four central questions about the future of the firm:

1. What will the organization of the future look like?
2. What will the office of the future look like?
3. What will the employee of the future look like?
4. What will the jobs actually be?

The conversations that we've included in the following pages tackle the biggest questions facing entrepreneurs today when they are facing *inward*—looking at themselves, their people, and the organizations they are building.

The Organization
Is the Product

ARI BUCHALTER, CEO OF INTERSECTION

Intersection has institutionalized disruption as an ongoing capability, taking the friction out of organizational change.

In my opinion, this profile contains what just might be the most important insight that you will find in this book. It comes from Ari Buchalter, the CEO of Intersection, a technology-driven advertising company that sits at the forefront of the smart city revolution sweeping the globe.

Buchalter has led three successful companies over a wide-ranging career that's straddled advertising, tech, and finance. When we ask him what's changed during that time, he singles out one idea: innovation cycles just keep getting shorter. Over the past fifteen years, he says, he's been shocked at just how quickly intellectual property that was developed at great expense has turned into a commodity just a few years later, as cloud services that anyone can buy for pennies on the dollar.

What are the implications of that shift? "The historical idea around entrepreneurs and innovation tended to focus on the product," he says.

"But what's happened is that *the organization has become the product*. That's the thing you have to nurture, because anything you build is going to become a commodity in two or three years—you just have to assume that's going to happen."

There, that's it.

But let's start at the beginning: Buchalter decided that he was going to become an astrophysicist when he was six years old. Twenty-five years later, it was the late 1990s, and he'd earned a PhD and was working on postdoctoral research.

"That's when I discovered that my love for the career didn't match my love for the subject," he says. "The equity markets were going crazy at the time, so in addition to studying the origin of the universe, I began studying trading and derivatives pricing." He even set up a small investment fund for friends and family. It didn't do so bad, but as Buchalter points out, in the late 1990s, you could have thrown darts to pick investments and still come out ahead.

Buchalter soon realized he had to make a choice—academics or business? He landed at McKinsey & Company in 2001, in part because management consultants seemed like the academics of the business world.

This was early Internet, when the term "new media" was in vogue, and Buchalter found himself entranced by opportunities to work with clients in the fledgling realm of big data, helping to answer questions like: *How do you segment your customers? How do you optimize pricing? How do you predict consumer behavior?* When it came to analyzing all that data, his skills as a physicist came in particularly handy.

In 2005, he joined a niche consultancy called Rosetta as head of its digital media and technology vertical. Three years and a liquidity event later, he cofounded a company called MediaMath, which offered a DSP, or demand side platform, to allow advertisers (and their agencies) to take advantage of an emergent category called "programmatic advertising." Ten years later, they'd built the company from ten to eight-hundred-plus people, and it was time again for a change.

Buchalter once again took stock of the state of digital innovation:

- Phase one, as he saw it, had been about "native online" advertising, or search engines, portals, and basic access to information.
- Phase two had been about connecting the online and offline worlds, whether that was buying products on Amazon, ordering cars through Uber, or renting via Airbnb.
- Phase three, he realized, was about changing the face of the physical world with technology, via the Internet of Things, self-driving cars, smart homes, you name it.

In his world—advertising—Buchalter saw a huge opportunity in public spaces. Instead of simple billboards showing giant, static advertisements, he saw a future where outdoor ads were going to be powered by a lot more of those characteristics that most of us associate with the online world—data, targetability, measurability, even interactivity.

At the same time, he was also hungry for a way to add a social-impact mission to his advertising expertise. That's when he discovered Intersection, an ad-tech company focused on smart city technology and connectivity around public services. The company's flagship product, LinkNYC, was already the world's largest and fastest free public Wi-Fi network, but Buchalter realized that the transformation of outdoor advertising was just beginning. He joined Intersection as CEO in May 2017.

So let's get back to the notion that *the organization is the product.* What does that mean? It means that you shouldn't spend all your time focusing on what you're building and how you can protect that competitive advantage—it's all going to get away from you in the end, anyway. (For more on this, see David Greenberg of Updater, page 53.) The point isn't that you shouldn't just try to protect what you've built—Buchalter is all for maximizing the value of your efforts for as long as possible—but you've got to focus just as much (or more) on building an organization that is perpetually able to see what the next wave is going to be, and to master the transition from today to tomorrow. In as *frictionless* a manner as possible.

"How do you institutionalize disruption as an ongoing capability?" he asks from a boardroom inside the company's sparkling headquarters in New York City's new Hudson Yards development. "I don't mean every day. You can't come into the office and plan to disrupt every Monday and Tuesday. But you have to have a homegrown ability to do it in two- to three-year cycles. And you have to train and develop people that have that growth mind-set. That's the only way to have an organization that's nimble enough to step onto the next S-curve."

Buchalter thinks the most compelling example of that kind of company today is Amazon. Jeff Bezos, he argues, has built a culture and a formula that says, "We understand how to solve our customer needs, and how to bring data to bear to do that, and we're going to take that formula from one discipline to another." He's right. Whereas Google has tried to institutionalize that ability to sidestep into new businesses, they're still a search company at the end of the day. Amazon, once *The Everything Store*, has become *The Everything Company*. "They're doing it at amazing scale," he says.

Under Buchalter's leadership, Intersection's strategy offers a compelling case study in the same kind of thing. Formed in 2015 when Titan Outdoor, a large player in outdoor advertising (including on New York City phone booths), merged with a technology and design company called Control Group, which was best known at the time for the rollout of tablets in airports, the two came together after they'd submitted the winning proposal to New York City's RFP, or request for proposal, regarding the city's aging pay phone network. The solution was LinkNYC, which isn't just about free public Wi-Fi. It's also the source of hundreds of millions of dollars of annual advertising revenue for New York City.

Today, Intersection is focused on using advertising dollars to kick-start a virtuous cycle of funding the rather expensive deployment of smart technology in cities all around the world. They've partnered with the Chicago Transit Authority (CTA), for example, to deploy the InTouch Kiosk, an interactive display with opportunities for a variety of advertising-driven partnerships.

Intersection provides a vertically integrated offering to its largest customers: the hardware, software, content, and information management, as well as the ad sales force. But in an acknowledgement that they will never own or operate all the screens in the world's public places—as well as one that allows for an adaptive response to disruptive innovation—they also offer bespoke parts of their proprietary technology stack to help power other people's similar solutions. In other words, they've got both a proprietary media business *and* a Software as a Service, or SaaS, business. They're well positioned, to boot: with traditional print, radio, and television advertising budgets shrinking in relative terms of overall spend, out-of-home is the only other form of media beyond native online that is growing.

Intersection's main product, in other words, is whatever its customers need it to be. That's a profound change from years past, when corporate identities were more resistant to change. When Buchalter arrived a few years ago, 90 percent of the company's top line came from traditional advertising. In a few years, he thinks, that proportion will have dropped to around half, with the balance coming from newer, licensing-oriented revenue streams.

"A lot of companies try to fight it, but you have to just let it wash over you," says Buchalter. "Understand that the march of progress and democratization of technology is unstoppable, take it as a given, and focus on your culture instead." Buchalter thinks that companies differentiate themselves the same way that progressive educational institutions do, by favoring a growth mind-set over a fixed one. He once replaced an entire technology team because of their inability to accept that a technology into which they'd invested untold effort had reached its expiration date.

At The Inside, I tell my product team the same thing all the time. There will never be a day when we can say that we're *finished* building our site. There will never be a day where we can sign on the dotted line and say, *This is perfect!* and move on. Buchalter agrees: "Early in my career, I suffered from the illusion that things get *finished*," he says. "Things get *done* but things never get *finished*."

Ben Lerer of Lerer Hippeau, one of our venture backers at The Inside, puts it like this: "Our most successful companies have founders thinking about things other than the day to day—the why the company exists, the what it's like to work there, the how they do what they do."

So how do you build an organization that lasts? How do you perfect *that* product? You need to try to avoid hiring people who will be frustrated by the fact that things are never finished, and find those who understand that flux is now the perpetual state of reality. You need to hire people who are *curious*, because if they're curious, they will keep looking for that next thing.

"I put less of a premium on experience and more of a premium on the growth mind-set," says Buchalter. The result? The average age of Intersection's employees has been coming down since his arrival, because youth always has a superior ability to pick up the next thing—

they don't have hard-coded preferences to do things a certain way. (*Young* is also a lot less expensive than *Experienced*.)

We can't all be doing new things every day. There has to be a period where everyone has sufficient understanding of where the next phase of the strategy is, says Buchalter, at which point, you put your heads down and get the job done. But you've *always* got to be thinking of the new ideas that will be coming in from clients, competitors, and the market, a lot of which will be pushing against your stated priorities. "In some cases, you will want to question the priority and maybe change it," he says, "but in most you will need to stick to your plan. You need to focus on execution over short time frames but keep yourselves open to continual disruption over medium ones. That's a tough balancing act to pull off. I think it's the hardest part of leadership."

He's right; it is. But today, it's also mandatory. If your organization does not become your product, then your product is eventually going to be defunct.

What Office?

ANDREA BREANNA, FOUNDER AND CEO OF REBELMOUSE

Andrea Breanna changed her business—and the world—by taking interpersonal friction out of the office. By making the dream of a distributed and geographically dispersed workforce actually workable, she also removed friction from the daily commute and gave us all back a little time as a result.

It's no surprise that a typical office setup was never going to work for Andrea Breanna, the founder and CEO of online publishing platform RebelMouse. One of the more prominent transgender CEOs in the start-up ecosystem, if not the country, she says she's never fit into boxes very well.

Breanna was a coder from the very start; one of the first things she coded was a Choose Your Own Adventure game in the 1980s. (Duff has written a Choose Your Own Adventure himself, *The CEO*.) After her father received an MBA from Stanford, he started a software company called Palo Alto Software. "In the beginning, every disk that the company sent out had a label that was put on by my eight-year-old hands," she remembers.

One of Palo Alto's products was business planning software for small businesses and entrepreneurs. In the early days, they sold through partners like Best Buy, and with that came the usual wholesale-retail nightmare of dealing with returns and getting paid.

But then, in the early 1990s, the Internet started to become real, and Palo Alto outfoxed the competition when it came to search terms on Google, and grabbed a 70 percent share of its market. "It was like a magical bottomless cup," she remembers. "If I could drive three hundred more downloads tonight, it literally costs us nothing more. The search phrases I won in the mid-1990s are still responsible for 80 percent of the company's revenue today."

But here's one key thing: it was at Palo Alto that she began working with people situated around the world. A pit stop at Avaaz.org (a sister site to MoveOn.org) followed soon after the turn of the century, where she helped build a 45 million-member community using a sophisticated platform and—again—a distributed team.

A burgeoning career as a coder followed, but Breanna's big break came in 2004, when Ken Lerer and Jonah Peretti offered her the job of chief technology officer at their fledgling Internet media company, Huffington Post. "Arianna is the public figure," she says, "but Ken Lerer was in many ways the founder of HuffPo. He's such a fun creative person to work with, but he's not an office-based person. We'd just get it done through phone calls, with quick feedback and no bureaucracy."

Breanna chafes at the unconscious biases in tech, such as the idea that you need five guys and a whiteboard to really get a company off the ground. An early-career stint trying to work remotely from Mexico didn't go well—no one wanted to hire a remote coder, even for twenty dollars an hour—so when she did ultimately return to New York, she decided to be the kind of person who was not blind to the talent of the world, something she thinks happens to 99 percent of people in New York, San

Francisco, and elsewhere. "And listen," she says, "my mother's mother, who I barely saw more than once a year in person, knew everything that was happening in my life, despite the distance. She even knew the night I lost my virginity. So the idea that distance could prevent you from being close never clicked with me."

Once ensconced at HuffPo, she started acting on her beliefs. She hired a coder, Nike Goren, who lived in the Ukraine. Some colleagues were wary at first, but the experiment worked, and before long, HuffPo was setting itself apart from the competition due in part to its distributed workforce. "Five guys and a whiteboard have to go to sleep," she says. "But in our model, you could set up among Europe, Asia, and the Americas teams, and they would pass the baton.

"We had a star in Turkmenistan who lived like a king on the salary we paid," she says. "He was the envy of all of his friends. Nobody would pay someone in Turkmenistan like I did." This being pre-Google Hangouts, when Skype was still one-to-one, the group did the majority of its communication through email and chat. When the company raised $25 million in its Series B funding, they finally brought twenty-five developers to New York so that they could meet each other for the first time.

When she started RebelMouse in 2012, it was obvious to her that the content management system, or CMS, paradigm of the era was broken. The limitations of CMS tended to result in companies driving engineers too hard, and the plan was to create a company that treated engineering talent the way she thought it deserved to be treated.

But she made a mistake: she caved and built a business model that matched what her venture capitalists wanted. The main thing that entailed was having *an actual office*, in the same building as Lerer Hippeau in New York's SoHo neighborhood. Success meant more hiring, which meant more office space, and before long the company was on the hook for $25,000 in rent, and their burn was nearly $800,000 a month. "Before long, it wasn't about who was the best person to have in the meeting or the best person to make a decision," she says. "It was about who was in the office."

She solved the problem by *shutting down the office entirely.*

The next thing she did was follow through on something she'd always wanted to do but hadn't had the guts to do until then. She'd always categorized people around drama and output. High-drama and low-output people never lasted. Low-drama and high-output people were keepers. But it was the high-drama and high-output people that caused real problems. One salesperson in particular created so much drama that Breanna spent about 30 percent of her time doing damage control.

"I thought the way to deal with it was to apologize for the toxicity," she says. "That settled my karma with some people who had to endure it and realized that I wasn't endorsing it—I was *apologizing* for it—but what I should have done was fire them. When we finally went to a no-office model, we got rid of all those people, because it stripped all the packaging off. If you're toxic in that environment, you won't last. Because you can't fake people out by being nice in the office. We got rid of all of them." (My strategy has always been to surround myself with people I can trust; I find that I need them for my sanity.)

Fast-forward a little bit, and Breanna met a CEO coach who taught her one of Warren Buffett's secrets, which is that there are no such things as "business" decisions—they're all *personal*—and therefore the way he makes those "business" decisions is by following the North Star of his own personal happiness. *What would make me happy?* So she started to do just that. "I fired a client who was horrible," she says. "The funny thing is, another client who was a competitor ended up paying us to drop that client anyway." She then took the idea to the entire management team and encouraged them to pursue their own happiness in business decisions as well.

"But can you really scale happiness," I ask her, "with a team of forty-six people?" She insists that the answer is yes. "We did have a lot of turnover in the transition," she admits, "but these days, when you look at RebelMouse people working together, they are usually having a ball versus being at each other's throats." She added another component from an investor in the company who told her that in his office culture, no one ever uses an escalated tone of voice, even in describing past challenges. People either know how to take it—and speak about it—in stride, or they don't. The latter don't get hired at RebelMouse.

"The corporate side of our lives shouldn't infringe on or eat up our personal lives," she says. "It should give your personal life more space." Today, with video calls the norm, Breanna doesn't expect everyone to show up happy to every meeting, which would be exhausting. But she does want them to make decisions based on what would make them happy. That includes her eventual coming out, in 2017, a prospect that terrified her but in retrospect was one of the more rewarding experiences of her career. The office has become even closer because of the honesty of it all.

So here's the thing: Andrea Breanna isn't just saying that a company with no office can be as effective as one with an office; she's saying that it's a superior model. "I guarantee you we are faster than any company with an office," she says. "I had so many entitled New Yorkers working for me before who loved the cool office in SoHo and the other young people they could lunch with. But they weren't there for the mission."

With no geographical limits, she says, they don't have to make sacrifices regarding who they hire. Instead, they will hire anyone, from anywhere, as long as they are great at what they do. And they mean it: "To do a deal with RebelMouse, you have to sign a deal with a trans

CEO, a very clearly out-of-the-closet head of revenue, and a woman of color who's the head of monetization," she says. "And almost everyone you meet is going to be a woman, LGBT, or a minority."

Today, they're in twenty-six countries, including Peru, Argentina, Chile, a bunch of European countries, and a bunch in Southeast Asia, including the Philippines, Singapore, and Bangladesh. "Our head of client services is in Serbia," she says. "She's so good. But I'm also positive that nobody was going to give her this opportunity." Last year, the company's top line grew by 80 percent.

One of the things that people don't talk about enough when they're talking about founding companies is that the greatest privilege isn't the chance to make money. It's to be able to touch so many lives, and hopefully in a really positive way. And the way I see it, it all goes back to the office itself. Breanna is creating something really special—it's fifteen to twenty years ahead of its time.

"Five years ago, when I mentioned remote teams, people would be like, 'Whoa!' And it would just like shock them. Today, everyone responds by saying, 'I wish we could do that.'"

The Power of the Pivot

CHRIS KEMPER, FOUNDER AND CEO OF PALMETTO

Chris Kemper's renewable energy company has had to pivot not once, not twice, but multiple times as it has faced multiple points of friction—from the pressures of its VCs to get big fast to the realities of an ever-changing marketplace. It's a case study in resilience.

When we got on the phone with Chris Kemper of Palmetto in late November 2018, he sounded relieved.

"I just got in from confirmatory due diligence with some investors today, so this is a nice break," he said.

"Boy, do I know the feeling," I replied.

"Yeah, it's tiring, isn't it?" he said. "We're on our Series B now. I bootstrapped my first company—it's a lot easier that way because you can stay focused on building sales and the organization. This part of it is just exhausting. It's a weeklong due diligence piece."

Kemper is no neophyte. He's been working in clean energy for twenty years now. After studying the economics of renewable energy in Ahmedabad, India, he worked as a management consultant for the World Bank, and eventually in investment banking at Goldman Sachs.

In the early days of renewable energy, the asset class drew a lot of investor attention because its "alternative" risk profile offered 20 percent-plus returns to those willing to navigate the government bureaucracy inherent in an industry that relied on accommodative policies to fuel growth as well as the adventure of it all. The first incarnation of Kemper's Palmetto was a London-based originator of such deals. And he says he enjoyed it, to a point. "It felt like we traveled to the edges of the earth," he says. "I've got more war stories than you can count, ranging from kidnappings to mass shootings at sites. I was once thrown in the back of a van and kidnapped myself."

But Kemper wasn't the only intrepid entrepreneur seeking returns in renewables, and the return profile eventually started approaching single digits. At that point, Palmetto version 1.0 was done. But Kemper wasn't. Thanks to the likes of SolarCity and other companies, the idea of residential solar as an asset was becoming better understood in the United States. He moved to Charleston, South Carolina, and started pitching peer-to-peer loans to people who wanted solar installations at home.

What Kemper eventually realized was that the most important reason consumers pulled the trigger on solar wasn't financing per se; rather, it was the feeling that they were dealing with a trusted brand.

So Kemper did what the other solar companies were doing: he tried to build a vertically integrated offering that could handle a solar installation from end to end; they did the marketing, proposals, financing, fulfillment, and construction. But that proved to be a financially unsound model—not just for Palmetto, but for everyone.

"The vertical model is a disaster," says Kemper. "And the reason we know that is because we did it." There are also the dead companies walking: SolarCity would be gone if Elon Musk and Tesla hadn't bailed it out in 2016. Sunrun, another early player, has public equity worth about $1.7 billion, not much more than the $1.4 billion in capital it has raised. "That tells you what the capital markets' view of the sector is," says Kemper. "It's hardly worth the cash that's been put into it; there's no enterprise value."

In late 2017, Kemper had been on the road raising money for seven straight weeks when a team member called and told him he needed to get back into the office. Nobody was showing up anymore. That's when he realized that it was time to start making the tough decisions that are the backbone of any realistic pivot. "I left that venture capital pitch and took the first flight back to Charleston," he says.

Things were really coming apart. Kemper began contemplating bankruptcy. His lawyer gave him Ben Horowitz's book, *The Hard Thing About Hard Things*. Whatever the future, he knew he had a bunch of hard decisions to make sooner rather than later. If he took too long, there'd be nothing left.

He'd put together a vertically integrated model, and he could take one apart. Using a fine-grained analysis of the business, he found that of three segments—marketing/sales, construction, and software fulfillment—only the software division made any money at all. The others were sucking cash out of the company at a terrifying rate—$7 million in just nine months. Kemper realized widespread layoffs were on the horizon.

Around the same time, a potential business partner asked if they could license the Palmetto platform. Palmetto's lawyer had said no, but Kemper overruled him and a week later signed Palmetto's first licensing deal. One week after *that*, the marketing partner had notched more sales than Palmetto had in the entire previous quarter using its own sales team.

"Based on that one data point, I decided to eliminate the entire sales team," he says. The construction group soon followed, and Palmetto moved into a smaller office.

The pivot worked. Palmetto went from being a vertically integrated provider of solar installations to being, more or less, a software company that helped individual contractors manage their own solar-installation businesses. It became a gig economy story.

Palmetto's primary customers these days are people trying to start their own franchises installing solar panels on the back of his brand. The company has a suite of services clients can choose from, including lead tracking, design, proposals, financing, contract, and an installation tracker. They even offer success coaches for those who need it. As for homeowners, those who buy Palmetto installations get an app that helps track energy savings.

Palmetto calls contractors who use its platform "alchemists." On average, they earn $68,000 a year, which compares *quite favorably* to an Uber model and other types of secondary, gig economy incomes. Alchemists love it so much that the company has grown without spending a dime on marketing—it's all word of mouth.

When we met him in 2018, the company was well on its way back to profitability. But unlike the majority of venture-backed startups, Kemper had decided to raise a significant amount of debt as well as equity, and to keep raising as much as he could of each. Why?

"Because I think there's a massive misalignment between venture capitalists and founders," he says. "Venture capitalists make twenty bets and they only need one to be a unicorn or even halfway decent. I'm interested in longevity as a brand, and to achieve that, we have to be around, financially speaking. That means I'm not going to take $6 million in equity and blow it on R & D to get to a Series B. I'm always going to have liquidity available to me, and I'm always going to be stockpiling cash."

Why is that? Because during Palmetto's dark year, the company nearly went bankrupt eight times. "I had a great boom, and then a great big bust, and then a great big boom, like many entrepreneurs," he says. "Luckily, I am seasoned enough that I was able to tell my investors that I would be bringing in debt when I brought in equity, and I would keep raising as much of both as I could, even though my Series A investors wouldn't like it.

"Raising money is just the start," he says. "After that, there are a whole lot of steps: You need to scale the business, generate positive free cash flow, hire the right talent, keep enough equity to keep interest, and maintain enough liquidity for the down times. When you look at traditional venture investing, it basically treats people like lottery tickets. That's dangerous; you'll be out looking for a job before you know it."

In January 2019, the *New York Times* reported that the message was getting out there: "[For] every unicorn, there are countless other startups that grew too fast, burned through investors' money and died— possibly unnecessarily. Start-up business plans are designed for the rosiest possible outcome, and the money intensifies both successes and failures. Social media is littered with tales of companies that withered under the pressure of hypergrowth, were crushed by so-called 'toxic VCs' or were forced to raise too much venture capital—something known as the 'foie gras effect.'"[2]

A lot of Series A and B investors have asked Kemper why he doesn't spend more on customer acquisition. "Because we're spending it on building a better product," is the reply. "Somewhere in the last decade, things like margins and cash flow models and business basics went out the door," he says. "People haven't cared about any of that because there's been so much capital around. But that's going to correct itself at some point. That's when they'll start looking at companies with strong organic growth again."

By late 2018, the company could count 1.5 million households that had been served by Palmetto-associated installers. It was highly solvent, grossing a million dollars a week; was profitable; and was in the process of building a great culture. Palmetto was on course for a $100 million annual run rate in sales by year's end. And by January 2019, Kemper had raised a total of $34 million, only $11 million of which was equity.

To recap: Palmetto got into the solar business just like everyone else, as a vertically integrated entity. But it didn't work for them—it didn't work for anyone—and the company nearly went bankrupt as the early enthusiasm around solar gave way to frustration and burnout due to the complexity of the still-nascent sector. Kemper saw an opportunity to reenergize the industry and fix a broken delivery mechanism. In other words, he saw an opportunity *to take the friction out of a broken model*.

"This is an industry where you need to be asset light," he says. "If even Elon Musk can't pull it off, with all his access to capital, I don't know who can." Kemper and his team are now focused on facilitating the gig economy around solar, making life easier for sales partners and installation partners. They recently launched Palmetto Bank, a $20 million credit facility to help partners get their businesses off the ground.

A Palmetto app for homeowners in late 2018 turned into a lead generation machine for partners as well. South Carolina homeowners who choose to go solar can earn instant savings on their utility bills if they do so through the app. How so? Palmetto takes 10 to 20 percent of, say, a $5,000 sales commission, credits it to the end customer, and then subtracts that from the commission it pays to the installer, to whom it ultimately gives a lead they would not have otherwise gotten.

A $4,000 commission is better than a $0 commission, so everyone is happy in the end. "In two weeks, we had a thousand new customers, all by word of mouth," he says.

In the end, says Kemper, it's important for entrepreneurs to know who they are and what their value is. "If your value is just super growth and you want to raise a couple of rounds and don't care, that's fine," he says. "But don't play by somebody else's rules. Stability is really important to me. I didn't know that at first, and I took dumb risks, and we hit rock bottom before I figured it out. Only then did I finally have the strength to disagree with my investors. There are some really powerful venture capital groups that put some very aggressive people on my board." Most of whom, we can only assume, have come around to Kemper's point of view.

The Frictionless Fit

ANDY DUNN, COFOUNDER AND CEO OF BONOBOS, FORMER SVP OF DIGITAL BRANDS, WALMART ECOMMERCE

What's the secret of Bonobos's success? Simplicity. The company's co-founders focused on the dead simple goal of making a better-fitting pant, without any further complications. In doing so, they removed friction from a process nobody even realized was fraught with it. They followed that with a frictionless way to market and then stores without inventory. By removing friction everywhere they could find it, Bonobos revolutionized the market for men's pants.

The following story might be the most surprising in this book. I'm not going to surprise you by telling you about a company you've never heard of. I'm going to do so by telling you something very surprising about one of the best-known companies on earth: Walmart. And about an entrepreneur who, like many readers of this book, would have laughed if you'd told him that he'd be working for Walmart one day. That entrepreneur is Andy Dunn, the cofounder of men's apparel brand Bonobos.

When I think of Andy Dunn's career, I think of a puzzle where seemingly independent pieces have come together to make one big, coherent whole. We'll get to the Walmart part in a bit, but let's start with the puzzle pieces themselves.

A graduate of Northwestern University, with a bachelor's degree in economics and history, Dunn's first job was as a consultant for Bain & Company. One of the clients that he worked for during that time was catalog-based retailer Lands' End.

"When I worked with Lands' End's call center, I saw the crazy connections you can make when you rip out the generally not-that-interesting brick-and-mortar experience and insert a direct relationship with the customer," says Dunn. "Later, when we were launching Bonobos, it was based on the premise that the Internet was going to be just like the catalog business, except better because you can personalize it." It didn't surprise Dunn in the least when Lands' End was ranked number two in J.D. Power's 2012 Online Apparel Retailer Satisfaction Report, second only to another catalog veteran, L.L.Bean.

After Bain, Dunn worked as a private equity analyst at Wind Point Partners. He worked on retail there, too, and the time spent at Wind Point solidified his love of working with consumer brands. "You get to think a lot about people and how they make decisions," he says.

Then came Stanford Business School. If it gives some readers hope that even the most successful entrepreneurs have some ideas that don't get off the ground, Dunn has *three* for you. He'd been noodling around with the idea of getting into the import business, bringing really cool things he'd discovered in other countries to the United States. "I know that's not a new idea," says Dunn, "but I was thinking I could build a whole venture capital incubator around it." His candidates: South African beef jerky, called Biltong; superpremium sippable rum; and a fast-food chain centered on falafel and hummus. "Falafel and hummus are the only things that people in the Middle East agree on," he says.

He went to one of his business school professors and told him that he wanted to start a venture capital firm based around the triumvirate. The professor told him it was a terrible idea. Biltong, for what it's worth, is illegal in the United States, as it's uncooked meat. Sippable rum was a good idea—Diageo, one of the world's largest producers of spirits, later bought the brand that had inspired Dunn's idea, Guatemala's Zacapa Rum. It was the fast-food chain, though, that earned the bulk of his professor's scorn. The upside of backing brick-and-mortar, inventory-driven businesses was not big enough to offset the downside of the losers for venture capitalists, he told Dunn, who was crushed.

Not completely deterred, Dunn spent the summer between his two years of business school working for the only venture capital firm he knew of that would invest in those kinds of companies: Maveron, created by Starbucks's Howard Schultz. At the end of the summer, when Dunn received an offer to join Maveron after graduation, he still harbored dreams of backing his Biltong business. But then the man who'd helped him get the summer job at Maveron in the first place told him not to accept the offer. Why? "You're an entrepreneur, not a venture capitalist," he was told. Dunn wasn't so sure about that—entrepreneurship seemed too risky to him—but the words resonated enough that he began wondering whether he did have what it took to be a founder, not just an investor.

Back at Stanford in 2007, Dunn's roommate Brian Spaly told him about *his* plan to start a business.

"I'm going to make pants," he told Dunn.

And why was that?

"Because pants don't fit."

Dunn was stunned. "I had all these big ideas and talked about them a lot," he says. "And there was Brian, who didn't talk nearly as much. He was just like, 'Pants don't fit.'" Spaly was an athlete and had what's known as "hockey butt"—small waist, big butt and thighs—and he could never find pants that fit. He ended up buying pants with too large a waist (and therefore the right-sized thigh) and altering them. So he'd decided he was going to make them for the masses, something no one in men's apparel had ever done before. That, dear reader, is what's known as a dead simple idea. And the Internet loves dead simple ideas.

A service trip to Kenya to help a family with their grocery store finally showed Dunn the light. That family's shower was a warmed-up bucket of water in an outdoor stall. Once back in Atherton, California, while standing under his double showerheads, he realized, "Fuck this. There's no risk in starting a company in the United States. Risk is not having health care. Risk is not knowing where your next meal is coming from. Having reflected on that aha moment, I came to believe that if you have the privilege to do something that spiritually excites you, you're kind of obligated to try." For the rest of our sakes, we should be grateful that Spaly and Dunn did just that. Because otherwise, there still wouldn't be pants that fit.

Spaly was supposed to have gone to a wedding in Brazil while Dunn was in Kenya, but he hadn't; he'd gone to Los Angles to buy fabric instead. "He had two sets of fabrics for each pant," recalls Dunn. "The outer fabric and a liner fabric. His insight was that we were going to have pocket liners that peek through in the back pockets that were really cool prints, so there was a little bit of wink in the product. He's super dapper. He took his altered pants to a pattern maker in San Francisco and she made him a pattern." They launched as an exclusively online brand in 2007. JetBlue chairman and Stanford lecturer Joel Peterson signed on as a founding board member.

Another thing Dunn had noticed while working with Lands' End was the idea of the long tail—the opportunity provided by the Internet to sell low volumes of hard-to-find products as well as large volumes of popular ones. Lands' End was selling into Sears stores at the time, having just been purchased by the struggling retailer. "We had this great pink cashmere sweater, which was a beautiful product," he says, "but we couldn't assort it anywhere because we don't sell enough pink cashmere sweaters anywhere in the country to know where to put it in what size. America buys enough pink cashmere sweaters in aggregate that someone like Lands' End should carry it, but at any given location, you couldn't assort it because there was never enough local demand. So you take out style and enthusiasm for cool stuff, colors, and prints, and then you also have to take out fit. Brian and I decided to solve for that with an endless aisle—we were going to out-assort from a fit, color, and size standpoint."

Dunn moved to New York with four hundred pairs of pants. When the orders came in, he packed and shipped them out of his own apartment. Within six months, they had a $1 million revenue run rate. But they kept it scrappy. Dunn says he found their first customer service reps on Craigslist by advertising for "customer support ninjas." (If that sounds overplayed in 2020, it wasn't in 2007.) Things just kept picking up speed from there. They raised $18.5 million in their first institutionally driven financing round in 2010, another $16.4 million in 2012, and another $30 million in 2013. Four years later, Walmart bought the company for $310 million. (We're getting to that soon, we promise.)

Looking back, Dunn says Bonobos can lay claim to three inventions. The first was a better-fitting men's pant. The second was a new way to build brands on the Internet. The third was retail stores without stock, the Bonobos Guideshop.

It's not a revolutionary idea today, but in 2011, Bonobos was one of the first online retailers to begin experimenting with a physical location that wasn't a store but simply a place to "try before you buy." The first Guideshop was in the company's New York City headquarters. Within two years, they'd opened nine.

Guideshop addressed the dirty little secret of online-only retail: almost no one in e-commerce makes money. "Online businesses are so hard because you have the costs of shipping, returns, marketing, and your team," says Dunn. "And your team needs to be an apparel team, a customer service team, a technical team, and an operations and fulfillment team. Add that up, add in the cost of promotions, free shipping and returns, and you have nothing left." Dunn even wrote a paper in 2012 called "E-Commerce Is a Bear."

What does make money? "Omni-channel makes money. If you can build a four-wall model that makes money, that can cover the losses of your e-commerce business. The reason the four-wall model can make money is that you don't have to spend on marketing because people still exist in the physical universe and, surprisingly, they go places to get stuff. So you get all this leverage on your fixed costs in brick-and-mortar that, in theory, could come with e-commerce. But it never does. Unless you hit some ginormous amount of scale, and you can sell other brands, you're not going to make money."

But what about all that talk about disintermediation—the removal of wholesalers from the supply chain by direct-to-consumer brands? That happened, says Dunn, but those middlemen were then replaced with new middlemen—Mark Zuckerberg and Larry Page, the toll collectors of the majority of e-commerce happening today. "With Bonobos Guideshop, we figured out that you just can't be online," says Dunn. "You need physical retail." He even coined an acronym to describe the idea: Digitally Native with a Vertical Brand, or DNVB.

In 2007, Dunn and Spaly had thought that owning their own brand would protect their margins enough that they'd eventually make money. The only problem was that "eventually" was actually a very big number—Dunn's own estimate is that you need about $200 million in sales to get there. Otherwise, the giants of e-commerce will *eventually* crush you.

"That's one of the main reasons we sold to Walmart," he says. "I was worried that being a public company would be really hard." Dunn knew that the news Bonobos had sold to Walmart wouldn't necessarily be cheered by everyone. The day of the announcement, Walmart stock fell 5 percent. "I'm looking at my iPhone," he says, "and thinking, 'Is Bonobos that bad of an investment?'" But it wasn't that: the very same day, Amazon announced that it had purchased Whole Foods, and the stock market took it as a sign that Walmart's grocery franchise was now at risk.

Here's where things start to get surprising: another reason that Dunn thought Walmart was the right place to be was because he thinks that the company is a force for good. Yes, you read that right: a company that many considered the poster child for *bad* corporate behavior in the 1990s has begun to refashion itself as a retailer that's doing right by its employees and the environment. What's more, having been trounced by Amazon when it comes to e-commerce, Walmart is now, unexpectedly, an underdog. And America loves its underdogs.

"What Walmart cares about is much bigger than what I've spent my life's work doing, which has been digital," he says. "They bought Bonobos because of that, but we sold Bonobos to them for reasons other than that it would ensure the company's survival."

Among them: Walmart's sustainability initiatives. Dunn's wife, Manuela Zoninsein, has been focused on sustainability longer than he has, and when he came home to try and convince her to move to Bentonville, Arkansas (at least temporarily), he thought an appeal to her passion would help. "Walmart is really progressive on sustainability," he told her. Her reply? "Listen, you idiot, it's the most progressive supply chain in development in the world."

"Walmart's work in sustainability is far bigger and more advanced on so many vectors than what we were doing at Bonobos," says Dunn. "Apparel is number two, after oil and gas, as the most polluting industry there is, so there's a lot of interesting work to be done in sustainability." He points to Project Gigaton, Walmart's initiative to reduce a gigaton of emissions from the atmosphere between now and 2025, as an example, but says there are many more. "The more time I spent with them, the more I realized we would be lucky to belong to what's nothing less than a once-in-a-generation transformation."

Dunn joined Walmart as SVP of Digital Brands, Walmart eCommerce, heading up the company's digital, direct-to-consumer brands, reporting to Marc Lore, president and CEO of Walmart eCommerce US. He was tasked with building or buying what he and Walmart CEO Doug McMillon call soulful brands. "It's not about the business," says Dunn. "It's whether or not the brand matters to the world."

The way Dunn saw it, the way to create those brands was to have independent, spirited teams able to do their own thing, with their own story, and a social purpose. "Could we create that inside Walmart?" he wondered. "Most people would say no, but that's the experiment we tried." In time, they landed on four: Bonobos, ModCloth (an indie vintage women's brand out of Los Angeles with a feminist tilt), Eloquii (a plus-size women's brand out of Long Island City), and Allswell (an internally incubated bed-in-a-box brand). The Allswell team doesn't work at Walmart corporate but out of a WeWork facility. Visit it, and it feels like a venture-backed startup, except they don't have to worry about fundraising. That's what Dunn did.

You can learn a lot from people who can see the world of e-commerce from a perch like that which Dunn held, and we asked him what trends he thought had come to an end, the places that we *shouldn't* be placing our bets anymore. He offered up two.

In direct-to-consumer brands, he pointed out that the early winners online were in categories where people hated the experience, like razors and eyeglasses and mattresses. "The bar is higher now," he said. "All the really broken categories have been done. And as customer experience problems get harder to solve, it may even amplify the issues around soul and passion because you have to be good at all the esoteric stuff. There's a lot left to do in fashion and beauty online, but I think the bar is much higher than it was."

"I wouldn't want to go into the multibrand business in e-commerce either," he added, "because you're going to be running right up against Amazon and Walmart and Target and Costco. Stitch Fix is cool, and Chewy is doing well, but I don't think there's a lot of room left in that. You could do niche plays, like a tennis e-commerce brand or fishing or golf, and you could build a $10 to $20 million business, but if you're obligated for a larger outcome due to venture capital, that's going to be tough."

Speaking of Amazon, Dunn wrote in 2010 that Amazon's market capitalization would soon surpass Walmart's. He was right. He now thinks that Wal-Market could leapfrog its younger rival once again. "This is going to be a clash of the titans," he says. As Dunn's barber told him after the sale to Walmart, "Andy, you're riding with the elephant now, but this guy in Seattle, he's an octopus." Dunn smiled as he thought about it: "That would be a great name for a book, wouldn't it? *The Elephant and the Octopus.*"

How long would he stick around to ride that elephant? Dunn said he was in it for the long haul. But he also admitted finding out the very same thing I found out when I went to Wayfair: "When you've been an entrepreneur, becoming an employee again is a really humbling journey," he said. "I'm like, 'Oh, I suddenly remember what it's like to be an employee. This is hard.'"

In December 2019, Walmart announced that Dunn would be leaving the company. The initial strategy didn't pan out as planned—Modcloth was sold in October—and Walmart decided that it would shift to an incubation strategy as opposed to an acquisition-based one. It was time for Dunn to move on to his next opportunity, and he handled his departure with typical grace. What's next? Only time will tell. But at least his pants still fit.

Chapter 7

THE FRICTIONLESS YOU

M ost of the entrepreneurs you've read about in this book are using the idea of *frictionlessness* to make their organizations more competitive, whether that's by improving the customer experience, the company's competitiveness, or the adaptability of the organization itself. We also came across a number that are working on the most important project of all—YOU.

How best to describe the seismic changes that are going on all around us, thanks to the forces of *frictionlessness*? You might say that the ground is moving beneath our feet. That's why Heidi Neck and her colleagues at Babson College have rejiggered the curriculum of their business education program to better prepare students for a future in flux.

And that's a good thing. Because founding and running a startup is pretty stressful. I've never done anything else that comes close. Putting The Inside together took a real toll on my health, and in the midst of trying to raise money *and* launch a business, I also found myself talking to a variety of specialists about intestinal permeability, or leaky gut.

One of the first things everybody asked was whether I drank too much caffeine. Guilty as charged. As a French Canadian, I've always enjoyed a little wine, too, but it soon became clear to me that like many things, our ability to withstand the effects of even a minimum amount of drinking starts to decline with age. Even so, cutting back on those two digestive evils didn't make me feel better. There had to be more.

That's when I discovered the whole concept of the gut biome and all the fascinating work being done around the "second nervous system." In short order, I began to hack my health. The forces of *frictionlessness* aren't just operating outside of our bodies; they've also allowed us to go more than skin deep when it comes to our own health.

Consider vitamins. Until recently, most of us took vitamins based on what our doctor recommended—Who *hasn't* been told they need more vitamin D?—and what we ourselves had concluded about our health needs. Well, that whole way of thinking is an anachronism. These days, you can design entire health-care regimens around the vitamins (or minerals, or whatever) that you're *actually* lacking. We can't actually see inside our bodies, but we're no longer fumbling around in the dark when it comes to our health either.

The rest of the entrepreneurs profiled in the pages that follow are focused on helping *you* live a better life. Gil Blander and Dr. Erika Ebbel Angle are focused on making it easier to calibrate your own health, from the inside out. The next, Alexandra Fine, is using the forces of *frictionlessness* to help bring much-needed parity to the world of sexual pleasure. Our final profile, Brandon Krieg, is helping *all of us* prepare for our eventual retirements, one dollar at a time.

The Courage to Learn

HEIDI NECK, PROFESSOR OF ENTREPRENEURIAL
STUDIES, BABSON COLLEGE

Heidi Neck and her teaching colleagues at Babson are way out in front of the seismic changes taking place in business today, offering students an education in the fuzzy front end of entrepreneurship—the places where there's still lots of friction to contend with.

Heidi Neck has been teaching entrepreneurship at Babson since 2001. So what's changed since then?

At Babson, a degree in entrepreneurship has historically been about new venture creation, she says. "But what our students learn is transferable. The world needs our students to think and act entrepreneurially, regardless of what they do."

We ask Neck about the value of a college education these days, when you can find pretty much anything you want about any topic you're interested in on the Internet. If all the knowledge is in the cloud, what point is there of a college campus?

"My favorite song is 'Landslide' by Stevie Nicks," Neck replies. "Google can provide you with the lyrics, but it can't teach you how to sing." Neck says the role of educators is to create environments in which students can actually experience and practice aspects of entre-preneurship. "Our job is to help students sing."

How have the changes that technology has wrought been reflected in the curriculum? What ways *can* they be reflected in the curriculum? "Given how the nature of work is changing," says Neck, "our job is to teach students how to act in increasingly uncertain environments. They need to get comfortable with the uncertainty of our age. Which means they need to develop the ability to *learn how to learn.*"

And for that, we might add, they will need to develop the *courage* to learn.

That's just as important—or perhaps more important—for those in the workforce today as it is for those who haven't entered it yet. Why? Because the technological revolution is rendering increasing numbers of jobs irrelevant with every passing day. You don't need to be on the forefront of technology to realize that call center jobs, once a mainstay of a consumer economy, are not long for this world. At this point, the first fifty questions a customer has can be answered by a chatbot. I know that because when I asked Britt to look into chatbots, she came back two hours later and told me that we were good to go—our chat-bot was already operational.

What's the difference between ambiguity and uncertainty? "To me, ambiguity means 'I'm a little confused, but I can figure it out.' Uncer-tainty, on the other hand, is more of 'I have no idea what the hell is going on, but I have to do something.' From an educator's perspective, we have to teach them how to 'act in order to learn,' as opposed to the old way, which was 'learn in order to act.'"

Neck teaches what she refers to as the "fuzzier front end of entre-preneurship." That's the stuff they can't jam into a spreadsheet—topics such as mind-set, idea generation, opportunity identification, and anal-ysis. What's changed in the past two decades? "More educators are emphasizing evidence-based entrepreneurship over writing a business plan," she says. "I'm not against planning, just against the *business plan* per se." The other thing she's seen is that the thing they're teaching has shifted from entrepreneurship to the entrepreneurial *mind-set.* What does that mean? "It means that some of the most impressive stuff is going on outside business schools themselves," says Neck. "Engineering schools are adopting it, there's entrepreneurship in the arts . . . everyone is much more accepting of the e-word than they were twenty years ago."

At The Inside, I ask my employees to act like entrepreneurs too. So much uncertainty and ambiguity have crept into every facet of business these days that it's not just the CEO of a startup that needs to be entrepreneurial—it's everyone. Those are the only people who are going to be adaptable enough to survive now that the once-steady ground that is business is literally moving beneath our feet.

But it's not just for startups either. "Twenty years ago, students who wanted to work for large companies were leery of taking entrepreneurship courses, because they thought that larger companies would be turned off by it," says Neck. "Today, it's the opposite—the large companies are saying, 'We want those kids, even if they're not going to be with us for a long time.' That's a big shift."

The thinking at Babson, says Neck, is that the teaching of entrepreneurship is a way to make sure that students realize that business cannot be considered as a collection of silos. They're trying to teach students to be *whole-minded.* "Every entrepreneur ultimately understands how marketing integrates with sales," she says, "how sales integrates with operations, and how operations integrates with the overall business model—because everything in business is connected." The goal? To provide graduates with the wherewithal to tolerate ambiguity and navigate uncertainty, and the ability to see the totality of a business.

While Neck teaches entrepreneurship in the context of starting a business, what she's really teaching, she says, is entrepreneurship as a life skill. We agree. If you're going to succeed at all in the future, the entrepreneurial mind-set isn't just something you might want; it's non-negotiable.

As every entrepreneur can tell you, of course, you can't teach the majority of the things that make for a successful entrepreneur. When we ask Neck about Harvard Business School's vaunted case method, she scoffs. "Students can't know how to navigate a system in real time until they actually do it," she says. "Case studies don't give you that experience." So what can business schools ultimately do, if they can't offer actual experience? "In some respects," says Neck, "I think we're giving the students the courage to try." Which is a lot.

Which company founded by a Babson grad is her favorite showcase of all that an entrepreneurial venture can be? That would be Bigbelly Solar, founded by Jim Poss. Bigbelly has applied both renewable energy (solar) and cellular communication to the complex and expensive process of waste collection. The company's sensor-equipped waste and recycling bins transmit real-time status to municipalities to streamline waste operations. In short, they don't come to collect the trash until they have to.

What does Neck worry about when it comes to her students' mindset? She worries that they all think they're going to start a business, get that $50 million in funding, and then exit the business with a stunning liquidity event in just a year or two. "There's too much attention on the exit," she says. "Young entrepreneurs need to focus on building a scalable business rather than a fast unicorn exit. If they build for scale, the exit will come at the right time for the right reason."

She's right. You can trust me on this too: entrepreneurship is just too difficult to enter into with a gambler's motivation. If all you want to do is roll the dice, go buy yourself some dice.

The CEO of Living Forever

GIL BLANDER, FOUNDER AND CHIEF SCIENTIFIC
OFFICER OF INSIDETRACKER

InsideTracker takes the friction out of staying healthy by telling you exactly what foods you need to eat to keep your body operating at peak capacity. By helping you calibrate your own well-being, they have taken prevention out of the medicine cabinet and put it in the refrigerator, where it belongs.

Gil Blander came by his life's work the way the luckiest among us manage to do: he figured out how to turn an obsession into a career. What was Blander's? The fact that he realized, at a very young age, that he was going to die one day. Pretty much everything he's done since has been aimed at making sure that doesn't happen. "I decided that my goal would be to live forever," he says. Color us impressed: as far as career goals go, they don't come much loftier than that.

After studying biology as an undergraduate, Blander completed his mandatory service in the Israeli army and then decided to find a good lab in Israel that studied the problem of aging. He couldn't find one, but he did find the Weizmann Institute, whose tagline "Science for the Benefit of Humanity" would seem a good indicator as to whether it was focused on solving the immortality problem. Not so. He did, however, find the man he considered the best scientist in Israel—Professor Moshe Oren—but Oren didn't study aging; he studied cancer. Impressed by the young Blander's quest, he told him that if Blander could find some sort of overlap between cancer and aging, he might be able to hire him.

A few weeks later, Blander presented his findings: a protein that had been identified as responsible for premature aging syndrome (also known as Werner syndrome) had been spotted hanging out with a protein that the cancer researchers were very interested in as well. That was enough for Oren, and Blander spent the next five years at Weizmann. When it came time to do postdoctoral work, Blander headed to the United States to research alongside MIT's Professor Lenny Guarente, one of the world's foremost experts on the science of aging. The original plan, circa 2002, was to get that piece of paper and then head back to Israel. He's still in Massachusetts today.

Why? Because Cambridge's Kendall Square district cast its spell on him. A fertile mix of corporate investment and academia—where employees of thousands of biotech companies rub shoulders with the Nobel laureates of MIT—it's the kind of place that attracts the best minds and then doesn't let them leave. In Blander's case, cosmetics giant Estée Lauder started sniffing around some of his work on the aging of skin, and the next thing he knew, he'd secured one of the largest fellowships in the history of MIT. "That's when I started to realize that I could contribute more to humanity if I started my own company than if I stayed a professor and published a few papers a year," he says.

Before he did that, though, he took a transitional gig at a systems biology company. During his downtime, he continued the quest. Example: it's been more than one hundred years since scientists showed that "caloric restriction" can extend lifespan—take any model organism and cut the amount of calories you feed it by 50 percent and it can live

50 percent longer. But we're still not quite sure why that is so. In pursuit of clarification, Blander built a mega-database of all the experiments that had been done on caloric restriction to see what might drop out the bottom. A couple of colleagues told him that he should quit his job and start a company around the whole idea. "I was naive enough to take their advice," he says.

Today, as founder and chief scientific officer of InsideTracker, Blander is at the forefront of the movement that begins with the premise that everyone is different and ends with the conclusion that generic health and nutrition advice is pointless for *actual people*. If you're going to try to improve your health, you need to find out what's happening inside *your* body and then derive *precise*, science-based recommendations from that.

It all starts with a blood test. Of course, there isn't enough blood in a human body to run all the blood tests that you *could* run on someone, so Blander and his team first set out to narrow down the number of blood biomarkers that they *would* test for. They began with one strict criterion: they are looking at biomarkers of *health*, not *disease*. "We're not trying to replace your physician," he says. "We are trying to help people that are currently healthy to become optimized. Because being normal is boring."

The second criterion was that the biomarkers must be amenable to natural interventions—food, supplements, exercise, and lifestyle—with observable effects. "I don't want to use drugs, and I don't want to use biomarkers that might tell me I will have dementia in twenty years, but that aren't actionable," he says. The final criterion was driven by economics—biomarkers had to point to something that at least 1 percent of the population is dealing with at any given time. In the end, they landed on about forty. From there, they compiled peer-reviewed research on those biomarkers, but again with an eye to personalization.

If you're going to target glucose levels in *your body*, in other words, it's anachronistic to think of yourself in the context of what you see on most blood test results: an *overall* range that covers *all people*. No, what you want is an *optimized range* that takes into consideration things like your actual age and gender.

It turns out that Blander isn't alone in seeking immortality. Inside-Tracker is working with everyone from marathon runners to CrossFit athletes to the military, Fortune 50 companies, and vitamin manufacturers. After starting with just blood tests, the company is expanding into other "layers" of information about your body, including DNA and activity trackers that tabulate things like heart rate, sleep, and weight. What *don't* they do? They don't offer to analyze your "gut microbiome" and send you recommendations based on that. The science isn't there yet, he argues, and any advice based on gut microbiome analysis is "premature." (We met someone, Dr. Erika Ebbel Angle, who obviously disagrees about that. We'll tell you about her when we're done with Blander.)

Does all this hacking of your own health really work? Blander says it does. Asked for proof, he points to a peer-reviewed study of one thousand users of the InsideTracker platform who employed more than five hundred customized interventions over a seven-month period. And guess what? Most of them worked. There were seventeen biomarkers for which at least twenty participants were out of the desired range at the start of the study, and almost all of them showed substantial improvement.

Here's a mind-blowing statistic to consider: when you consider the entire universe of food items that any of us *might* eat (InsideTracker tracks eight thousand), the average American consumes just twenty in any given week. But that's not horrible in and of itself. What is? Consuming those same twenty food items, *week after week* and *year after year*. We are unhealthy because of our abysmal eating habits. But the answer isn't to chase that Big Mac with a prescription drug for cholesterol. It's to make better decisions about what we eat in the first place.

"Our idea is to move the drug cabinet from the bathroom to the refrigerator," says Blander. He even offers himself up as an example. Blander says he always hated beans, but when his own product showed him that if he wanted to optimize his glucose and cholesterol, he should probably get over his distaste and start eating them, he did, and . . . started liking them.

You won't find InsideTracker advertising on Facebook. Why? Because Blander says this is a much more serious and complex topic than to be subjected to the whims of whatever the self-appointed nutrition expert in your friend group has to say about it. And that despite the fact that some of their findings are as prosaic as this: InsideTracker is building its own data set on top of the data sets it has collected, and in analyzing that, it has found, quite clearly, that people who eat takeout or in a restaurant at least once a day have much worse biomarker levels than those cooking and eating at home.

Duff: "We need to do this."
Christiane: "God, my biomarkers are going to be terrible."

Gil Blander is still planning to live forever. But he says he's expanded on that mission too. "My goal is to serve the ten billion people that will be on the planet in 2050," he says. We naturally wish him the best of luck.

Go with Your Gut

DR. ERIKA EBBEL ANGLE, COFOUNDER AND CEO OF IXCELA

The science of studying our gut biome is pretty cutting-edge stuff. But Dr. Erika Ebbel Angle's Ixcela is bringing the fringe to the mainstream, and taking the mystery out of dietary supplements—which should you take and how often—in the process.

As far as Dr. Erika Ebbel Angle is concerned, everything in her career can be traced back to the suicidal crocodiles. When eleven-year-old Erika visited a crocodile farm during a family vacation, she was stunned to learn that when crocodiles are mortally wounded, they expedite nature's work by simply flipping onto their backs and slipping into a coma. In other words, they kill themselves when all is already lost.

That was the same year Michael Crichton's *Jurassic Park* was released. She loved it. That led her to Richard Preston's *The Hot Zone*, and to subjects like genetics and immunology. Then came her first science fair. While the rest of us were busy building Play-Doh volcanoes out of baking soda and food coloring, little Erika Angle wanted to know the answer to the following question: Can individual cells commit suicide when they're infected by viruses to protect the greater organism? Put another way: Are we more or less advanced than crocodiles?

This being pre-Internet, the eleven-year-old scientist was forced to call actual laboratories using an actual telephone to see if they'd help her figure out the answer. Some of the labs she called turned around and called her parents, asking if they knew what their daughter was doing. Most just ignored her. But somewhere about twenty or thirty calls in, she got a *yes* from someone who worked in a lab not too far from the family home. His name was Michael Nachtigall, and he was director of the San Mateo County Public Health Laboratory. "He stayed after work to help me," she says, with the same amount of amazement such an act of selflessness would still cause today. "He spent time with me, gave me stacks of books to read, and told me to come back and ask questions. What a wonderful human being."

Dr. Angle went back to that same lab, year after year, and credits Nachtigall with putting her on the road to becoming the scientist she is today. After crocodiles, she upped the ante and began studying a plant that seemed to hold promise for treating the herpes simplex virus, the cause of cold sores. She expanded on that project for several years thereafter, working for a number of biotechnology companies along the way. When it came time to complete her PhD, for which she developed an investigative tool for discovering blood-based biomarkers for Huntington's disease, she was already familiar with some of the devices she would use to do so, including mass spectrometers. "The connection between childhood and adulthood is supercritical," she says. "That, and what Bill Gates has been telling us for years: all you need is one person to say yes to you, to allow you access to something you otherwise would not have, and it can change your life." At both companies Dr. Angle has run, she's hired children as interns. That, friends, is how the circle stays unbroken.

Fast-forward: Dr. Angle went to the Massachusetts Institute of Technology, or MIT. In addition to being brilliant, she's not too hard to look at, either, and won the Miss Massachusetts title in the Miss America program in 2010. While attending a Miss Massachusetts event at the VA Hospital in Bedford, Massachusetts, the hospital's head of research told her that there was someone she ought to meet, an entrepreneur named Wayne Matson. The two hit it off, and Angle, who was graduate school–bound, although undecided as to where, applied to the PhD program at the Boston University School of Medicine because Matson had just landed an appointment there himself. "I got into Caltech, but decided to stay on the East Coast—my parents were so disappointed," she recalls. "But I couldn't pass up the opportunity to work with Wayne."

Never heard of Wayne Matson? Well, perhaps you've heard of lead poisoning? Back in the 1970s, when the world first learned about dangerous levels of lead in our blood, Dr. Matson developed the first lead-poisoning tests for children. He holds more than one hundred patents. Matson is a devotee of "actionable diagnostics and therapeutics"—meaning, he's not content to theorize, but wants to see the benefits of his research in action. But until he met Dr. Angle, he hadn't landed on the idea of what you might call a "consumer" application of his work.

Over the course of a distinguished career, she says, Matson had come into possession of some remarkable data, on everything from neurodegenerative diseases (ALS, Parkinson's, Huntington's, Alzheimer's) to diabetes, heart diseases, all the cancers, concussions, depression, anxiety, and more. When the two sat down to look across those data sets, they saw that there was a subset of molecules that showed up again and again, as risk factors for certain types of diseases, disease progression markers, or just general markers of health and wellness. And the majority of them were microbiome-related, meaning they were either secreted by certain types of bacteria in the gut or regulated by the gut in some way.

"Take serotonin," says Dr. Angle. "Most people think serotonin is found only in the brain. But most of the serotonin in your body—90 to 95 percent of it—is secreted by enterochromaffin cells in the intestines. If you have an intestinal problem, it's likely you have a serotonin problem as a result. And if you have a serotonin problem, there's a greater chance of emotional imbalances. A lot of people know about the central nervous system, and the interconnectivity of limbs and muscles and nerves. But nobody ever talks about the enteric nervous system, which connects your gut to your brain."

Some people do talk about these things, of course. Consider the whole probiotics craze. Most of the participants in it are companies and marketers throwing money against something without necessarily knowing what they're doing.

"Why don't we start a business where people can take a simple at-home blood test that will inform them about their diet and nutrition, and possible courses of action, including taking specific supplements?" Angle asked Matson. "A test that's informed by science rather than by superstition, hearsay, or blind guessing."

All of which brings us to Ixcela. It's approaching that kind of stuff with a science-based attitude. You send the company a couple of drops of blood via pinprick, and they send you a report back that includes everything from meal plans to exercise plans to sleep plans. They also send you any supplements you might need. Imagine that—taking only the supplements you *need*.

The "metabolomic network" is a complex thing. We don't know everything about it. What we do know is that there are biomarkers reflecting metabolomic/genomic interactions and that by testing the microbiome/metabolome in the gut, we can gain insight into what therapeutic actions might be available to reduce chronic disease risk while contributing to an improvement in overall health.

Here's the thing, though: it's not like the advice that Ixcela offers customers is particularly proprietary. The majority of clinical data on biomarkers, as well as the implications thereof, isn't either.

What is? The process for collecting and analyzing blood collected from pinpricks. And that's harder than you might think. Remember Elizabeth Holmes and Theranos?

"At one point, my staff was joking that another blonde CEO who liked to wear black turtlenecks was getting a lot of public attention," says Angle. "At the same time, despite its innovative concept, our scientists were baffled as to how in the world Theranos could be doing what Holmes was claiming to be able to do: to conduct, on the spot, hundreds of tests on a single drop—about *five* microliters—of blood. We didn't think it made scientific sense. Well, it turned out we were right. It might be possible to do that 30 years from now, but the technology simply doesn't exist today." For its part, Ixcela collects multiples of that—seven or eight drops, or *thirty to forty* microliters—and only runs eleven separate tests on it.

More than a few microbiome companies have come and gone, many of them because consumers were misinformed and thought they'd purchased a silver bullet to perfect health, when what they'd actually bought was just a baseline, something to compare themselves against in the future. It's only after two or three months of intervention, she says, that you can see dramatic changes in your gut biome, though you may start feeling changes in overall quality of life sooner. "Why do we have a subscription program?" she asks. "Sure, it's great for revenues, but retesting is also the only way to know whether your interventions are working."

Ixcela's subscription program runs $140 a month. That's not cheap. But neither is a single bottle of high-end probiotics from Whole Foods, which can cost up to $60.[1] The good news is that it comes with advice. And even if your most health-crazed friends already do yoga and meditate and walk for thirty minutes a day, not everyone does. Human beings can largely take direction well if they feel that they understand it. If the cause is X and the result is Y, and Y is going to be improved health and a better life, most of us, I think, would be willing to take the steps to do so, provided they don't feel insane.

But what would the crocodile do?

The Business of Orgasm

ALEXANDRA FINE, COFOUNDER AND CEO OF DAME PRODUCTS

Alexandra Fine changed the narrative—the one that said women didn't care about innovation in sex toys. By using Kickstarter to fund a company no one wanted to touch and then social media for frictionless marketing, she brought democratization and gender equality to yet another under-served community.

Alex Fine wanted to be a sex therapist when she grew up. Like so many of us, she was fascinated by the taboos around sexuality—the fact that we're not supposed to talk about certain things in polite company. "I thought being a sex therapist was the only way to really validate my interest," she says. To that end, she got her master's in clinical psychology from Columbia. The only problem with her education? It taught her that she's not a good listener and she's also very impatient.

She ended up scrounging around for a job and landed at a small consumer goods company based in Scarsdale, New York, that sold natural shampoo for kids. The job was a crash course in small business management—how to go from concept to product, about sourcing and distribution—and it gave her the idea that maybe she could start a business herself. She soon had the opportunity, as well, because she got herself fired.

The origin story of Dame Products smacks of kismet. Fine had landed on an idea for a tiny vibrator that could offer controlled clitoral stimulation during penetrative sex. All she needed to do was figure out how to design something that would nestle into the vulva and stay put during sex—something superior to her own prototypes made out of quarters and rubber bands. And for that, she needed an engineer—preferably one with a vulva herself. "The idea was that they could try the prototype out themselves, and fix it based on their own experience," she says. "So it didn't *have to* be a woman, but it would obviously be helpful."

A year and a half into searching for someone, she'd pretty much given up trying to find a product-design engineer who would deign to work on sex toys. That's when someone said to her, "I met your cofounder the other day." The same thing started happening to Janet Lieberman, an MIT-educated mechanical engineer, and Fine's eventual cofounder. Before long, the two connected, went out for breakfast, and got "business married" on the first date. That same thing happened to me at The Inside, with my cofounder Britt Bunn. Sometimes, you just know when you've found *the one.* You don't have to be *actually* married, à la Charles and Ray Eames. You just need to know you're on the same page.

Fine had taught herself 3-D printing and gave Lieberman a prototype to try out. Within a week, Fine remembers, Lieberman had redone six months' worth of Fine's amateur design efforts and came up with something close to what Eva would debut as—a tiny, egg-shaped vibrator with even tinier wings that tucked into the labia to hold it in place. I read somewhere that the two cofounders had credited OXO kitchen products as design inspiration, and you can see it quite clearly—the curves are beautiful, and the toys would not stand out in a kitchen drawer.

Within six months of meeting, the two were ready to go with Eva and launched a crowdfunding program on Indiegogo. They raised $575,000 in forty-five days. They weren't giving away equity, just discounts on the product itself, which officially went on sale in 2014. Early sales were really strong—Dame has sold more than 100,000 of Eva and its successor, Eva II. That's when Fine realized that there might just be a huge community of people that were dying to have the same conversations she'd wanted to have for years.

Dame found no shortage of willing product testers. When they were designing Eva, they made changes as small as two millimeters in response to customer feedback. Duff and his girlfriend, Joey, are Dame product testers. They tried Dame's wedge, Pillo, which helps you find the perfect angle in a variety of sex positions. When we tell Fine that's how we came to Dame Products in the first place, she doesn't censor herself: "That's fucking awesome!"

According to Fine, some of the best ideas for new Dame Products have come from customers themselves. They asked their community, "What's your favorite toy? And why?" and then made a word cloud from all the whys. "I used to try to code the qualitative information," she says, "but now I just visualize it. One thing we realized is that our customers don't want an app to go with their sex toy. They just want a simple product that is designed to be invisible.

"This is an important conversation," she says. "And not having it is as damaging to society as having it could potentially be—there are some issues that aren't going to get better by not talking about them." When it came time for their second product, the seventy-five-dollar Fin—a tiny vibrator worn snugly in between two fingers, in a hands-free kind of way—they raised $394,000 on Kickstarter, and were the first-ever sex toy company to use the site. "People gave us so much support and so much feedback," she says. "They were so excited to be a part of our process and support our mission. In sex toys—especially sex toys for people with vulvas—word of mouth is *everything*."

That's because of the double standard. Which double standard? The one where New York City's transit agency accepts ads for men's erectile dysfunction drugs showing a cactus representing an erect penis, but flatly rejected Dame's effort to develop the first-ever subway ads for vibrators. In June 2019, Dame Products filed suit against New York's MTA in US District Court in Manhattan with the goal of leveling the advertising playing field. It might not change the MTA's mind.

But the sanctimony isn't limited to the MTA: Facebook won't let the company run ads. Neither will Twitter. When the *New York Times* wrote about her, Fine linked to the article on Facebook saying, "I'm so honored to be in the *Times*." Facebook shut that down too. You'd think they'd be more focused on getting all the hate and fake news off the site than keeping a lid on profiles of bold, young, female innovators, but Facebook is mystifying that way. One of the most money-hungry companies in history, willing to sell your data to anyone who's got a dollar, they nevertheless find female sexuality is off-limits. So it goes.

"What's really interesting about the taboo is that no one is ever, like, 'Oh, I have a problem with vibrators,'" says Fine. "It's always them being worried about how *other people* would feel. But everybody realizes that the opportunity and the challenge are the exact same thing. It's all about the taboo, and changing the taboo."

That leaves, "press, press, press," according to Fine. "Even though people don't want our money, people really do like talking about sex, so good stories in the press can go a long way." When Megyn Kelly had Fine on her short-lived talk show on NBC, Fine managed to get the words "clitoral stimulation" out on national television. "It was really awesome," she says. "Thank you, Megyn Kelly." More recently, Dame has moved into a realm that most high-performing direct-to-consumer brands are in, and that is producing its own content, including sexual horoscopes and a frequently updated blog.

Why crowdfunding? Because while the world's largest tobacco and gun companies have public market investors aplenty, the markets are notoriously prudish—up until recently, there was only one publicly traded company in the porn business. And also because the venture capital industry is one of those industries with a lot of older, white men in it, and they didn't feel comfortable talking to a couple of twenty-something women about vibrators. It hasn't gotten a whole lot better since: "While #MeToo has changed the conversation in a really positive way," says Fine, "there's definitely a group of people who are even more uncomfortable than before; they're so *confused* about sex now, especially if it's related to work.

"There is a pleasure gap when it comes to enjoying sex," says Fine. "And heterosexual women rank lowest." She's not kidding: recent surveys show that heterosexual women are four times as likely as men to say that sex has not been pleasurable at all for them over the previous year. "There's also the orgasm gap," she adds. "But both are just quantifying something we all know to be true."

In today's e-commerce-for-everything era, it shouldn't surprise that sex toy companies do brisk direct-to-consumer business, given the privacy factors involved. But Dame found willing wholesale customers, too, including Urban Outfitters, Free People, Revolve, and Gwyneth Paltrow's Goop. Dame sells on Amazon too. But Fine says they're willing to meet their customers anywhere they feel comfortable. "I want you to have a completely branded experience that redefines what sexual wellness and pleasure and tools can be," she says, "and that takes that discussion beyond the sticky floor of the traditional porn shop.

"I don't know if this is true for everybody, but it's true for us," says Fine. "When we started this company, we became activists for our purpose. And some days, it can be really hard, because the forces holding us back include the fact that people think that the taboo isn't really hurting anybody. But it is." An informal industry group, Women of Sex Tech, has worked together to get collective press for their efforts.

In the end, Fine wants people to start having those conversations that might be a little uncomfortable at first. She'll even go first, if that helps: "The Eva II is a little annoying to me," she says. "It fits differently for everybody. If I put it in at the beginning, it definitely stays in place. But once we're real slippery, trying to get it to stay put is pretty hard. And then sometimes I literally have to do cartwheels to get it to come out."

Alex Fine didn't end up becoming a sex therapist, at least in the typical sense of the term. She's delivering a different kind of sex therapy, though, and to a far wider range of people than the kind the other people with that master's degree tend to offer.

That's because Alex Fine isn't just an activist; she's a pioneer. How many sex toy companies have *ever* been started by a woman? Fine says she gets a little flak from Gen Z, because for them, gender is an illusion, so a woman-oriented sex toy company is an illusion too. "Yeah, okay, that's fine," she says. "But we still have vaginas. That's not an illusion."

No, it's not.

One Penny at a Time

BRANDON KRIEG, COFOUNDER AND CEO OF STASH

Brandon Krieg made saving money and exercising fiscal responsibility a frictionless task. Stash is dead simple, and everybody in the value chain wins.

In 2015, Brandon Krieg was already a successful entrepreneur. He'd cofounded EdgeTrade in 1996, which gave institutional investors direct access to so-called dark pools of securities (as opposed to through a broker), and sold it to Knight Capital Group in 2007. He ran electronic sales for Knight for a few years and then decamped to Macquarie Securities Group as head of global electronic execution. But something was gnawing at him—specifically, the fact that Wall Street was fundamentally unfair to small investors looking to meet their own investment goals.

With EdgeTrade, Krieg had leveraged technology to help large investors trade more efficiently. What he wanted to do next, he says, was bring a similar kind of technology-driven leverage to the little guy. But he (along with his eventual cofounder, Ed Robinson) didn't quite know what form that would take. They decided that the best way to begin would be by literally asking people on the street what they needed.

"Every time we asked someone about money or investing or savings, they all said the same thing," recalls Krieg. "It was, 'I really don't do it, I can't invest, because I don't save.'" Pressed further, the men (and women) on the street explained that the main reason they didn't invest was because *they didn't think they could.* Why? Because they weren't "rich." In other words, the people who need to invest and save for retirement the most weren't doing it because they thought it was something only rich people did.

The company that eventually became known as Stash—a digital investment platform for the 100 million or so Americans that have effectively been excluded from financial services—was built on three principles. The first one is financial education, something that is sorely lacking in American society. The second is that everybody deserves financial advice. The third is the insight that the best way to build a savings and investment plan is to make it habit-forming. "Think about it like weight loss," says Krieg. "You don't wake up tomorrow and decide to lose thirty pounds. You start with the first pound, then you celebrate it, and then you move onto the next few. Eventually, if you work hard at it, you will lose the thirty. The same principle holds in investing."

Stash helps small investors start small—with as little as five dollars a week—and go from there. Whereas most investing platforms require customers to buy full shares of investments, Stash breaks them down into fractional shares to get to that five-dollar minimum. At this point, the company has 3 million customers putting away an average of $1,432 a year through its Auto-Stash app, and also offers Stash Retire for contributions to Roth and Traditional IRAs. And they did it by making the whole process *frictionless*—by leveraging critical technologies to democratize an industry in need of disruption.

The goal is to help the 80 percent of Americans who live paycheck to paycheck find a way to set some of that aside. And they seem to be doing a good job of it: 84 percent of "Stashers" are first-time inves-tors. The company's Stock-Back program rewards debit card customers with stock in various companies that they might buy from, including Walmart, Amazon, and Starbucks. Stash Cash Back skips the stock part and puts cash back into customers' investment accounts. And the debit card is paired with a zero-hidden-fee bank account. Finally, the company's custodial offerings allow parents to open custodial accounts on behalf of anyone under eighteen, to get them started early.

Stash's raison d'être, Krieg says, is the fact that banks have aban-doned those customers at the low end of the income and wealth spec-trum. "Next time you have a chance, go into any bank—it doesn't matter which one—and say, 'Hey, I really want to start putting some money away for my future. I have fifty dollars. Can you help me?' See how it goes. People need a new kind of company to help them with these problems. That's the most important thing we're doing."

An alternative rationale: consider the fact that checking account overdraft fees are a $20 billion business in the United States alone. The average Stash customer currently pays about $360 a year in banking fees, and 30 percent of them pay more than $70 a month. What does all of that add up to? It means that Stash is taking on the traditional banks, which are constantly in search of new ways to skim money from their customers' accounts.

Are Krieg and Robinson just trying to get those fees for themselves? They insist that they are not. Krieg says they're not focused on assets un-der management, for the simple reason that their clients don't have a lot of money in the first place—the last thing he wants to do with Stash is to take it from them. Rather, the company makes money by charging cus-tomers a subscription fee—just $1 a month for accounts under $5,000 and 0.25 percent of assets for those with more.

The irony of this is that the mission has resonated with the very

players that Krieg thinks are unfairly advantaged—institutional investors. Since its founding, Stash has raised over $116 million from the
likes of Coatue Management, Union Square Ventures, and Goodwater
Capital.

It hasn't been all smooth sailing. Krieg and Robinson embrace a
philosophy that allows for "micromistakes" while also leaning on data
science to help the company learn fast from them. Corporate missions
come and corporate missions go, but this one seems likely to stick: helping the least well-off among us do a better job saving for retirement, all
for just one dollar a month. Brandon Krieg can make all the micromistakes he wants; he's on his way to making a macro-difference.

Chapter 8

FRICTIONLESS SYSTEMS

n 1970, the economist Milton Friedman wrote an essay in the *New York Times Magazine* titled "The Social Responsibility of Business Is to Increase Its Profits." His argument was the opening salvo of what would come to be known as shareholder capitalism. Flouting the midcentury view that the best type of CEO was one with an enlightened social conscience, Friedman claimed that such executives were "highly subversive to the capitalist system."[1]

While Friedman still ranks as one of the greatest economists of all time, this particular idea has long since been rejected by society. It's even been rejected by the business establishment and academia. In the May/June 2017 edition of the *Harvard Business Review*, Harvard Business School (HBS) professors Joseph Bower and Lynn Paine published, "The Error at the Heart of Corporate Leadership,"[2] in which they argued that Friedman's view was not only outdated, but wrong. "[The] insistence that corporations . . . cannot have social responsibilities and that societal problems are beyond the purview of business (and should be left to governments) results in a narrowness of vision that prevents corporate leaders from seeing, let alone acting on, many risks and opportunities."

It's an admirable turnaround from the nation's most prominent business school. But in coming to that conclusion, HBS was simply catching up to the rest of society. While the pressure to please shareholders is as intense as it's ever been, the founders of many of today's most successful startups have internalized the idea that corporate profits and social responsibility are not opposing objectives. They are both essential, and some would go so far as to say they are both mandatory. An increasing number of institutional investors feel the same way—so-called impact investors, their mandates require them to invest in companies that are aimed at both shareholder profit and societal benefit, and not just the former.

The conclusion is as blunt as Friedman's misguided dictum from the 1970s: today, you can't just start a company. You have to consider its impact on society as well.

That's not so intuitive in my world. I'm shipping big pieces of furniture. So I've had to ask myself: What do I do to make an impact that's actually real? Do I give away a portion of sales? Or do we do something like sending all of our furniture returns to homeless shelters? Whatever we ultimately decide, the mandate for social good is just that—a mandate. This used to be something you could consider as a sort of add-on to your corporate purpose. Today, it's part of the table stakes.

A reporter who recently wrote about The Inside got it all backward, suggesting that because we're competing in the furniture industry's version of fast fashion, we were going to be producing too much stuff. Wrong. We're "fast" in getting design trends to market, but we don't actually *make* things until they're sold. So it's not just that we're not going to produce lots of product that might not sell; we're not going to produce *any* product that doesn't sell. We are *fast* and *responsible,* able to offer unlimited selection *without* a warehouse full of goods. The textile industry, of course, is notorious for its environmental impact. But new manufacturing technologies have changed that, too, both on the environmental and consumer health sides. It's pretty amazing stuff.

Millennials are demanding corporate social responsibility of the companies they work for or do business with as customers or partners. According to Deloitte, 42 percent of millennials have begun or deepened a business relationship because they perceived a company's products or services to have a positive impact on society. Further, 37 percent said they have stopped or lessened a business relationship because of questionable corporate ethical behavior.[3] Consider the speed with which media companies dispensed with misbehaving men in the wake of the *New York Times*'s explosive exposé on the behavior of movie mogul Harvey Weinstein.

And the more successful you are, the more—not less—pressure there will be from customers to conform to a corporate code that reaches well beyond the pursuit of profit. "Multinational companies in particular are more likely to combine their support for globalization with the espousal of wider societal goals such as protecting the environment, ethnic diversity, and gay rights," announced the *Economist* in November 2017. "A small but rising number of firms have committed to a new corporate purpose altogether, declaring their objectives to be broader than mere profits. The past decade has seen the launch of 'benefit corporations' which work to meet specific goals for society as well as for their investors; there are more than 2,300 of these around the world, with the greatest number in America."[4]

And it isn't just that you have to say and do the right things.

If you're busted for hypocrisy on this front, the penalties can be swift and severe. In December 2017, mattress startup Casper found itself on the wrong end of a federal lawsuit after it emerged that the company had been using software from an outfit named NaviStone to illegally collect information from visitors to the Casper website in order to learn their identities.[5]

Executives at Casper denied the allegations, saying that its online advertising practices are "standard" in the industry. But that's not good enough. After NaviStone's business practices came under scrutiny earlier in 2017, customers such as Wayfair and Road Scholar quit using the software. If they want to keep getting a good night's sleep in the future, Casper probably won't be far behind.

Casper, for its part, spent much of 2017 trying to explain its way out of questionable practices, and the software imbroglio wasn't the mattress retailer's only PR misstep. Just a few months before, news emerged that after suing a handful of mattress review sites for not disclosing that they were funded by Casper's competition, Casper pulled an about-face and funded the purchase of one of those very sites, Sleepopolis, potentially putting itself in "the awkward position of engaging in similar business practices to those it just sued."[6]

The poster child for misbehavior by a startup, of course, is Uber. News of the company's unethical business practices started with a drip, but by mid-2017 had turned into a torrent, with new revelations landing with disturbing regularity. Uber presents a number of lessons to any founder. The first is that the fish stinks from the head. You have to live your corporate life flawlessly today; words are not enough. This is really important to consumers. You have to constantly be asking yourself, "Are we still in alignment with our values?"

No one is going to demand that you save the world with your

startup. And you are pretty much free to outline the contours of your company's social mission yourself. Just don't be a hypocrite. Because if consumers will reward those companies that they deem to be on mission, they will likewise punish those that they do not.

But it goes even further than that. Increasingly, companies are being asked to make people feel good for buying their product, and in ways that aren't even about the product itself. It's not just about what they're buying, in other words, but who they think they are. That's where the newly pervasive concept of community—in the corporate context—comes from.

Can you do good while also doing good *business*? Of course you can. But I'm not telling you something you didn't know: the majority of us are well aware that decency and profit can go hand in hand. The following profiles will present several ways that founders are doing so today.

The corrosive idea that the two goals are somehow mutually exclusive may go down in history as Western capitalism's worst contribution to the fate of humanity and the planet itself. Thankfully, only the most stubborn members of the capitalist class (including their academic henchmen) have yet to let it go. In August 2019 the Business Roundtable even issued a joint statement saying that its members had abandoned the idea that shareholder interests were superior to all others. (For more on this, see Duff's book *The Golden Passport*. His response to the about-face: "It's about time.")

The forces of *frictionlessness* have freed the impulse to do something worthwhile from the shackles that narrow-minded capitalists put on it more than a century ago. You *can* do the right thing at work, and you *can* do it all day long. You just need to choose to do so.

On a related note, I am obviously elated to acknowledge that strong female leaders are finally having their moment. The women in this book serve as resounding proof of that fact.

One of the worst-kept secrets (among women, at least) is that in many businesses, women are doing—or could do—a better job than their male counterparts. Of course, I'm not talking about *every single woman*—generalizations are horrible in either direction. But I am talking about competence and capability in the field of business, and where you can find it. In days gone by, you weren't supposed to look for it in women. But information has been set free—made *frictionless*—and it's hard to obscure the fact that some of the most capable business operators working today are women.

The following profiles showcase a group of people working on some of the most exciting projects I talk about in this book. The first three are trying to solve one of the most pressing problems we have, which is the intersection of climate change and food. How will we feed ourselves without destroying the planet? This is important stuff. The final four are solving system-level problems for the betterment of us all. Would that we all could say the same thing about our efforts. I stand in awe of every single one of them.

Can I Put It on My Spaceship?

MATT BARNARD, COFOUNDER AND CEO OF PLENTY

It's hard to think of something more frictionless than vertical farming. Matt Barnard and Plenty make it possible to grow delicious food without dirt, pesticide, pollution, or residual crop damage. Some ideas are so revolutionary that unless someone acts on them, they won't exist. Plenty is one of those ideas.

Matt Barnard's staff made him a T-shirt of his favorite due diligence question during a recent financing round for Plenty, the vertical indoor farming startup he cofounded: CAN I PUT IT ON MY SPACESHIP?

It wasn't a joke: Plenty has *at least* one investor who owns their own spaceship—Jeff Bezos.

Barnard says there are three threads that brought him to the place he currently occupies at Plenty.

The first is the water system. Barnard has always been fascinated with large, system-level changes. The global water system has been an obsession for years, and at one point, he even raised a private equity fund to invest in water technology, all toward the end of solving the stresses that we're putting on the system. "The thing that struck me the most was this imbalance between the dire and epic and historic stresses the water system is under and the level of societal consciousness about it," he says. "People still use the resource freely without even thinking about it."

One thing Barnard learned during the private equity effort was that agriculture accounts for 70 to 80 percent of all water use, so if you're going to solve for the water system, you need to solve for agriculture.

Barnard is also obsessive about food. "I love cooking," he says. "I love finding ways to match food with people—I tend to view dinner parties as a puzzle." Barnard grew up on a farm in Wisconsin. The family sold apples and cherries commercially, and had its own massive garden for personal consumption. Whenever they bought produce at the store, his reaction was the same—"What is this stuff?" For years, he thought that he didn't like tomatoes or watermelon, which don't grow in Wisconsin, and therefore only came to him via the grocery store and had the flavor of the grocery aisle, not the garden.

And then there's health. Several years ago, Barnard was diagnosed with an autoimmune condition that supposedly wasn't curable. But by embracing a diet of fresh and plant-based foods, he rid himself of the condition entirely. A few years later, his wife was diagnosed with a rare form of breast cancer, stage 4 triple positive, and was told that it wasn't even worth treating. Eighty percent of patients die within five years of such a diagnosis, but Barnard's wife is in complete remission today. She responded well to treatment, and the couple believe she did so in part due to changes in her diet—they reduced the presence of inflammatory foods and increased plant-based portions. "Food is medicine," he says.

So back to that system-level stuff. Barnard points out that the current global food system is designed to work for about 2 billion people. The only problem? There are 7.5 billion people on earth. When Barnard and Plenty cofounder Nate Storey conducted a project on the entire global food chain, from seed to the home, to try to figure out what technologies were implied by the solutions the system was calling for, they landed on indoor vertical farming. In 2014, they put a farm on the Google campus and supplied the company's flagship cafe. "The chefs loved us," he says. "They were getting three to four times normal shelf life. They had to prepare less and throw away less, and people loved the food more."

It's hard to beat that for an initial demonstration of concept—the Google people have a way of getting their views in front of more than a few of us—and since then, Plenty has evolved into larger-scale farm systems that will allow the company to serve nutrient-rich foods to more people in more grocery stores across more income deciles. "Nutrient-rich and diverse diets have strong correlations with longer, healthier, happier lives," he says. "So that's what we're looking to solve for."

Plenty has experimented with growing about five hundred different crops. At the moment, they sell about a dozen commercially, including kale, tatsoi, and mizuna. They've got two facilities—one in South San Francisco, near the airport, and another in Wyoming. Barnard says the Wyoming facility is also the world's largest artificial intelligence plant-science training center, where they're learning to grow plants more efficiently, optimizing for yield, energy consumption, and flavor. The plan is to start placing these farms around the world while keeping the food costs as low as possible.

Agriculture, says Barnard, is a manufacturing industry. It doesn't matter, he says, if you do it outside, in a greenhouse, or fully inside—it's still manufacturing. Put in those terms, outdoor farming is hard because you're running a factory with no roof and no control. "So we've brought it inside to impose full control," he says. And they've found that plants can be made to be far more efficient than they've ever been out in the fields—grow much faster, taste far better, and have richer nutritional value. That's why you won't find Plenty competing head-on with your local farm on too many crops: things currently grown outside are chosen for attributes like stability and reliability and resilience to environmental change; Plenty selects for flavor and nutrition. "It's a completely different set of criteria to optimize around," he says.

When I tell him that I remember the lettuce I tried in Berkeley as tasting "clean" and "bright" with distinct flavors, Barnard isn't surprised. "It's funny you say that," he says. "I never thought to describe food as 'clean,' but that word keeps coming up. It's a common reaction."

When Dominique Crenn, who has earned three Michelin stars for her San Francisco restaurant, Atelier Crenn, visited the Plenty operation, says Barnard, she came in very skeptical. But she left saying, "How do you get your kale to taste like this? I don't even eat kale, because I can't stand it, but I love this."

So can you actually put it on your spaceship? "We haven't worked to solve for that, specifically," says Barnard, "but so long as you have power and water and a supply of nutrients, you should be able to grow anywhere." Here on earth, Barnard thinks Plenty can have the most significant impact by helping expand fruit and vegetable production from the few places where it's truly productive outside (the Mediterranean, California) and make it local where it's never been.

What does a Plenty grow room look like? Think of a hallway 130 feet long and 16 feet tall, with plants growing sideways out of the "walls." That's half a football field long and two stories tall. The company uses a hybrid soil/hydroponic/aeroponic system. There's both data science and machine learning in play to help plants optimize their photosynthetic process. And there is automation and robotics to help with transplanting and harvesting. (As the tractor might be to an outdoor farm, robotics is to the indoor one.) They use LED lights, which Barnard says have allowed Plenty the ability to give plants their "ideal" lighting, from spectrum to intensity and duration. They use sensor technology, per the Internet of Things. And they use cloud computing, running the farms from anywhere.

If that sounds like Barnard has somehow wrapped every single tech buzzword into one company—data science, machine learning, robotics, IoT, cloud—that's because he has. But he's also used them to productive ends. When they first put that farm on the Google campus, they achieved eleven crop cycles a year (versus just the one for outdoor lettuce). Today, they're getting more than thirty. With all those technologies coming down in price to the point of commodification, Barnard says he saw the potential for Plenty four years ago, he saw it become commercializable two years ago, and is seeing it becoming commercializable at scale today.

Is this the future of farming? Instead of asking people to be stooped in a field, they're asking them to be skilled technicians and technologists and logistics professionals. They still need "growers," who tend to the plants, but they can do so in such a leveraged way that the majority of an indoor farm's workers are of the former sort, not the latter. Barnard says the newest version of its farms, called Tigris, is producing more than 350 times the amount of leafy greens that current farms can grow.[7]

It should come as no surprise, then, that technologists have been among the firm's most ardent backers. The firm received a $200 million investment from Softbank, as well as contributions from the investment funds of Jeff Bezos and longtime Google CEO Eric Schmidt. Mike Gupta, the former CFO of Twitter, joined Plenty as CFO.

Is Plenty friend or foe to the world's organic farmers? "We have a complicated relationship," says Barnard. "They see us as both a threat and an enabler." Some of the world's largest growers of leafy greens and berries have inquired about the possibility of buying networks of

Plenty farms due to capacity constraints. At the same time, groups of independent growers from Vermont have asked the USDA to strip Plenty of its certification as the only organic indoor grower in the world.

So let's get back to water. According to Barnard, Plenty uses less than 5 percent of the water that traditional agriculture uses and less than 1 percent of the land. Whether or not you think indoor growing is the answer to our food, water, and climate issues, you can be quite sure that the percentage of fruits and vegetables grown indoors is going to rise in the years ahead. Barnard's ambitions aren't small either. "It took Amazon twenty-five years to get to the point where they could serve this many people," he says. "It's going to take Plenty a while to expand as well."

Eating Our Way Out of This Mess

**BRENT PRESTON AND GILLIAN FLIES,
COFOUNDERS OF THE NEW FARM**

Talk about a noble cause: at The New Farm, Brent Preston and Gillian Flies are removing the friction from our interaction with the planet itself.

Fifteen years ago, Brent Preston and Gillian Flies were the kind of couple that most of us know and some of us actually *are*: urban professionals aware of the growing threat of climate change and concerned that their individual efforts (recycling, avoiding plastic bags) weren't moving any needles and therefore didn't amount to much more than egoism.

It's what they decided to do about the quandary that sets them apart: they walked away from successful careers in media and international development to start an organic farm. Preston documented their journey in his remarkably engaging autobiography, *The New Farm: Our Ten Years on the Front Lines of the Good Food Revolution*. Famed restaurateur Daniel Boulud summarizes the book quite well, calling it, "A must-read story told with honesty, humor, and humility by a passionate farmer who reminds us what our food system can and should be about."

But the operative words in Boulud's description are *can* and *should*. The problem is that just because we *can* and *should* do something doesn't mean we're going to do so. Flies gave a TED Talk in late 2018— "We Can Eat Our Way Out of This Mess"—in which she discussed the future of climate and, by extension, humanity itself. Watch that, and you're likely to find yourself seesawing between hope and despair. Tackling them in reverse order . . .

The sources of despair:

- If we were to stop 100 percent of all global carbon emissions today, it would take two hundred years for the CO_2 in the atmosphere to return to 1970 levels. *Two hundred years.*
- More than 30 percent of global farmland has been "desert-ified"— turned from arable farmland into desert due to poor farming.
- The UN estimates that with current farming practices, we have less than sixty harvests left before the rest of the earth's farmland will become severely degraded or destroyed.

The sources of hope:

- There are growing techniques that can reverse the flow of carbon out of the soil and into the atmosphere.
- Some of those techniques require *less* work for farmers, not *more*, including reducing tillage, eliminating the use of chemical fertilizers, and allowing animals to graze rather than keeping them penned up in feedlots.

Why hasn't this happened?

Problem #1: Farmers who reduce their inputs and increase their outputs will obviously make more money, but *other* people will make less money off of that farmer. And the system has been built so that *lots of other people* profit off of the farmer—makers of pesticides, machinery, and genetically modified seeds.

"The fundamental reason these techniques haven't been adopted faster and on a larger scale is that they're inherently *low-input* systems," says Preston. "And we've got an agricultural system that relies on and profits from selling agricultural inputs. If your future system is one that eliminates the need for those inputs, it's hard to get anyone with money to start promoting the idea."

Problem #2: Most farmers are growing the wrong kinds of crops anyway. The majority of industrial farms grow what are called "commodity crops," the largest of which (in North America) is corn. In a really good year, with cooperative weather (which leads to high yields) and decent prices, a farmer can gross about $750 an acre growing corn.

The New Farm consistently grosses *more than $40,000 an acre* growing vegetables such as salad greens and cucumbers by hand. "The gross won't tell you how profitable we are," says Preston, "but it will tell you a lot about how much money every acre of our farm puts into the local community and how much wealth it's generating."

But let's get back to that part about less work. When they switched from tilling the land to a no-till system, Preston and Flies saw their lettuce yield jump by 25 percent. Not only that, the new crops had *far fewer* weeds, which meant a further drop in labor.

Problem #3: The way we currently measure the "profitability" of farming is too narrow to tackle a problem of this magnitude. "Money shouldn't—rather, *can't*—be the only currency by which we measure the 'profitability' of our land," says Flies. Some others: soil health, biodiversity, and community.

"We've only got about twelve years to start pulling the carbon back out of the atmosphere if we ever hope to survive as a species," says

Flies. "At this point, for farmers, sequestering carbon is more important than growing food."

The next step for The New Farm is to increase their footprint. Their original idea was to buy nearby farms and start new forward-thinking ventures on the newly acquired acreage. The only problem? Land is expensive.

So instead of buying land, the current plan is to lease it from wealthy weekenders—meaning, urban professionals like the ones Preston and Flies used to be who want to feel like they're doing something to address the overall climate situation. Better yet, current indications suggest that it won't necessarily be The New Farm paying landowners to farm on their land, but landowners paying The New Farm to do so.

Their initial plans include a grazing operation that uses regenerative grazing techniques that help sequester carbon—using smaller fields, lots of trees, keeping the animals on the land rather than in feedlots, feeding them grass instead of grain.

So what about the digital revolution? How have organic farmers like The New Farm managed to incorporate digital tools into their operations? Because growing crops is, well, a pretty analog affair.

Here's what they've done:

- They've helped spread the word via the Internet and social media. See KissTheGround.com or TED Talks like the aforementioned one Flies gave in late 2018.
- They're using the power of the media to help push emerging ideas like that of the "agrihood"—a new kind of neighborhood that facilitates farm-to-table living by integrating a working farm (instead of, say, a pool or a golf course) into a residential neighborhood— for sustenance to keep them on their sometimes lonely course.

- They've gone political, advocating for a carbon tax and national (and global) support of regenerative farming.

"It's time to stop wringing our hands and waiting for the world to end," Flies says in her TED Talk. "We all have a role to play; it's not somebody else's responsibility. The time for sustainability is past. We can regenerate. Let's eat our way out of this mess."

Trillion-Dollar Triage

SANJEEV KRISHNAN, CHIEF INVESTMENT OFFICER OF S2G VENTURES

Every big system has its points of friction, and the food system is no exception. By investing in new business models, Sanjeev Krishnan and his partners at S2G Ventures are hoping to eliminate these chokepoints.

It wasn't too long ago that Sanjeev Krishnan realized where he was going to make his mark. In 2013, consumers had already shown an inclination to use their pocketbooks to force a variety of industries to change their ways. First, they had embraced pioneering direct-to-consumer models wholeheartedly, wiping out wholesale margins in various realms. But in 2013, they were turning their attention to the food sector, where $1.2 trillion worth of entrenched business models were up for grabs.

"Consumers were starting to vote with their pocketbooks around sustainability and health," he says. Words like *organic, micronutrients*, and *traceability* were becoming pivotal integrated issues, not just theoretical siloed ones. "We decided to focus on a couple of multibillion-dollar niches, layer on risk capital, entrepreneurship, and innovation, and translate that into affordability, consistency, safety, and convenience."

The immodest goal: to help usher in an era of food where nutrition and affordability are pursued together, not as diametrically opposed choices.

If that sounds a little vague, this might be more specific: S2G Ventures is focused on investing across the entire food value chain, from agricultural, ingredient, and processing logistics technology to food processors, brands, and restaurant retail concepts. So far, the company has about forty investments that, when combined, effectively "mimic" the value chain, giving the partners at S2G insights into demand and supply signals, where there is market failure or opportunity.

They use multistage investing—seed, venture, and growth investing—so as to participate along the entire lifecycle of the *new*. New food technologies, he explains, unfold along lines similar to other "tough" technology sectors such as power, water, energy, and transportation—adoption cycles are long, the capital needs can be significant, and the channels are just as likely to be "physical" as they are "digital." This is not investing in consumer Internet technologies like PayPal, which can scale almost without human intervention. Food, by its very nature, is both seasonal and physical—you can't send improvements in code out every week or month and be done with it. "We need to be multistage so we can support startups through multiple cycles," he says. "We can't just assume that their technologies will be adopted in a sprint-like fashion. It's more of a marathon."

But what makes S2G intriguing is its "systems approach" to investing, which has implications for overall portfolio construction. What does that mean? S2G has a "cluster" around produce, for example. That means that when they're engaged with a produce giant such as Driscoll's or Taylor Farms, they can have discussions that may affect four or five companies at once without invoking competitive issues. Or, they make "force multiplier" investments: S2G has invested in a crop insurance company called Crop Pro Insurance, for example, which might have the potential to "de-risk" several of their ag-tech investments in one fell swoop.

They also look for synergies between portfolio holdings, and whether they can act as vendors or partners with each other.

One of S2G's investments, Midwestern BioAg (MBA), is a leader in high-yielding organic grain production that's been around for about thirty years. The company's proprietary products and processes allow farmers to grow organic grains and soys at parity with conventional farming costs. And Midwestern BioAg, which has five thousand farmers, more than a million acres of farmland, and 92 percent repeat revenue, also helps them get that product to market.

Another S2G investment, Mercaris, has created a data and trading platform for buying and selling organic non-GMO and other "identity preserved" commodities. Here's where their synergy comes into play: MBA helped Mercaris by encouraging a bunch of their customers to use the Mercaris platform; in turn, Mercaris helped MBA with merchandising.

Go one step further down the line, and you have Terramera, which produces high-performance, EPA-approved, organic bio-pesticides that help organic farmers with fungi and weed issues. "Our investment was driven by the belief that bio-pesticides and bio-fertilizers are the next frontier for sustainable agriculture," says Krishnan. Terramera is also working with MBA's customers.

Underlying it all is one question: How can S2G help bend the adoption curve to better facilitate long-adoption changes that may seem "inevitable" in light of major trends but which face various short-term hurdles due to entrenched industry practice? "If these problems were easy to solve, they would have been solved ten or twenty years ago," says Krishnan. "That's why systems thinking is important—you have to have a different mental model to disrupt some of these sectors in the physical commodity world than you do in the digital world. Software can't eat three-dollar corn. You have to have a much more holistic view of the market and the value chain in the way you do portfolio construction."

In addition to systems thinking, S2G has also brought about one hundred strategic coinvestors along for the ride—the fund has coinvested alongside Sumitomo, Syngenta, Tyson, Kellogg, and Whole Foods. Why are incumbents on board to stoke such change? Because they, too, can see that consumers are driving changes across the value chain, and they want to be waiting for them when they get where they're trying to go.

This is no small affair: Ninety of the top one hundred food brands have lost market share since 2015. And of the largest nine hundred new food brands since 2015, 88 percent of them emerged from small or medium-sized companies. In a marked departure from years past, consumers are now moving toward brands that Krishnan says cater to their "tribe"—paleo, vegan, keto—as well as local, natural, and clean label foods. In food, size is no longer the same guarantee of success that it used to be.

"Consumers are the most powerful force in the world, bigger than the capital markets," says Krishnan. "They account for 70 percent of US GDP, so the ways they vote with their pocketbook are the principal causes of change." The risk to a venture investor, of course, is that it invests in a *fad* as opposed to a *trend*. A fad becomes a trend when it's underpinned by demographics, culture, the media landscape, science, technology, and other things.

What does Krishnan think of Amazon's purchase of Whole Foods? It's obvious, he says, that Amazon is expediting the digitization of the "last mile" of grocery, and history shows us that some serious changes in market share happen in the context of digitization. (Think Netflix.)

The "first mile"—which includes farmers and their inputs—may be less amenable to rapid digitization, but that's happening, too, as inventory and shelf space move from their historical physical manifestations in actual supermarkets to the "shelf space" online. There's a reason that Unilever bought Dollar Shave Club, says Krishnan. They don't want to sit around getting disrupted by the likes of Amazon, and are instead hoping to find their own path to the consumer. The same thing is going to happen at various junctures in the food system.

But Krishnan and his colleagues are focused on problems that are even bigger than the existential threat posed by Amazon. They are looking at the convergence of health-care spending and national security, due to the fact that various branches of the armed forces have had to lower physical standards due to obesity rates. They are looking at how to help the food system move from its focus on producing cheaper calories to producing cheaper nutrition. And they are looking at helping capitalism evolve to something a little more humane than it was in version 1.0, when the dividing line between philanthropy and private enterprise was a little too bright—you were either doing one or you were doing the other. The world's food system is both at once—a profit opportunity like no other that needs to be entirely rebuilt just to satisfy our basic human needs.

"What makes me most optimistic is that this new generation of entrepreneurs doesn't see a false choice there," says Krishnan. "They embrace the friction."

And thank God for that. A lot of venture capitalists aspire to create something bigger than their own thing, and one way they try to do so is to yank disparate companies in the supply chain together to make something real happen. The problem is that most of them underdeliver in the end. But we're not going to solve the *really* big problems unless we try. If not for organizations like S2G, who are investing in different nodes in the food system and then trying to tie it all together, much-needed change would invariably happen at a much slower speed, and the *friction* Krishnan speaks of would just stay there, holding us back from doing the things we need to do.

Changing the World from the Bottom Up

**JIMMY CHEN, FOUNDER AND CEO OF PROPEL;
AND HANNAH CALHOON, COFOUNDER AND
MANAGING DIRECTOR OF BLUE RIDGE LABS**

Few realms contain more friction than your typical big government program. Consider food stamps: imagine if we all had to stand in line at the DMV every single week just to feed our families. By dragging that program into the twenty-first century, Jimmy Chen is doing God's work, giving valuable time back to the people who need it most. And Hannah Calhoon is funding every Jimmy Chen she can find.

One of the most common critiques of institutional investors in cutting-edge technologies these days is that too many of the companies they back solve for the problems of the world's elite—how to get faster video download speeds, how to get a taxi in twenty seconds or less—rather than, say, the more pressing problems of the rest of the world, including those living below the poverty line.

Too many, but not all. Take, for example, Hannah Calhoon, cofounder and managing director of Blue Ridge Labs, an initiative of the

Robin Hood Foundation that asks how technology can help unlock new ways to fight poverty. Calhoon and her colleagues at Blue Ridge are focused exclusively on helping nurture new ventures that are addressing the challenges faced by low-income New Yorkers.

Her professional path to Blue Ridge Labs is one of those journeys that makes sense in retrospect. A graduate of Harvard College, she spent her early career at consultancy BCG, eventually finding a spot on the firm's global health and development team, working primarily with foundations, aid agencies, and international NGOs. She soon real-ized, though, that no matter how good your intentions, if you're working on developing solutions for people who live in different geographical, social, and cultural contexts than yourself, it's practically inevitable that you will make poor product design choices at some point. She left the consulting world in 2014 with the goal of finding a gig with more local implications. A stint volunteering with the Blue Ridge Foundation in New York (the former incarnation of Blue Ridge Labs) led to an offer to helm the foundation itself when the executive director left for a job with New York City, and the opportunity to convince the trustee of a new direction.

Her starting premise was that tech could be an amazing force for change in lower-income communities if we just took the levers we were pulling to help upper-income people find more time in their lives and used them for the people who really need those five minutes back—the person already working two jobs and raising three kids in the process. "We asked ourselves why those platforms didn't exist," she says. "Why are there five versions of Uber-for-Laundry and no versions of a platform that helps a single mom who needs emergency child care and can't find a sitter?"

She knew intuitively, she says, that there were a lot of passionate folks in the start-up world who wanted to solve bigger and more important problems. At the same time, those with the technical skill sets and the access to capital to start new ventures tended not to have any experience—or even any interaction—with those very problems. That's where Blue Ridge Labs was going to come in—to create the bridge and find the ways to bring really talented people who wanted to be tech founders and focus them on a community-centric design process to discover ideas for new products and services to help people unlike themselves.

"Low-income people are just people," says Calhoon. "They have the same needs for products and services, and sometimes slightly different versions of those products and services because they have a slightly different set of constraints. There's a meaningful portion of our population that has a smartphone but not a data plan. So teams have to think creatively about if you're going to build an app how do you build an app that only downloads when people are connected to Wi-Fi or if they don't have broadband in their building. Or if you're thinking about a platform that's primarily for folks who are non-English-speaking workers and their primary form of communication with each other is WhatsApp. It's just different versions of problem-solving with different sets of design constraints. None of them are impossible, they just require a little bit of creativity."

They ran their first twelve-week class in the summer of 2014, with three ventures.

The first, Alice Financial, tackled pretax benefits for hourly workers, automatically adding those charges on credit or debit cards that should be pretax back into a company's payroll system. All-in, the app gives hourly workers an effective one-dollar-an-hour raise via pretax benefits without requiring employers to pay any more out of pocket.

The second, Yenko, is a platform that hooks into college information systems and helps students via a series of proactive nudges if they start exhibiting behaviors that might imperil their financial aid eligibility. Many of the grants and loans relied on by students in community colleges require students to maintain both minimum GPAs and course loads, and the app helps them realize when they're drifting close to either line.

The third, Propel, is a mobile banking app for managing food stamps and sourcing coupon benefits. Founder Jimmy Chen worked at both LinkedIn and Facebook before realizing that he wanted to spend his time and skills addressing something more important than consumer software. He wanted to fight poverty.

Specifically, he wanted to help the 40 million people who use food stamps in this country take maximum advantage of their benefits. And when he visited a food stamp office in Brooklyn and saw one hundred people waiting in line to see a human caseworker, that's when the light went off. This wasn't a hardware problem—75 percent of food stamp beneficiaries have smartphones—but a software one. So Propel started by building a website that made it easy to apply for food stamps.

Food stamp benefits are deposited on debit cards called EBTs. By asking users about their pain points, Chen and his colleagues discovered that EBT users had to call a phone number to check their balance—there was no software-enabled solution for doing so, despite the fact that EBT cards are used for $70 billion in transactions each year. That wasn't just a pain in the butt; it was also a source of anxiety—if you don't have enough on your EBT card for a particular batch of groceries, the whole transaction fails, and before you know it, the cashier is telling her manager (in front of everyone) that there's a problem with a food stamp customer. And so the folks at Propel built a smartphone app called Fresh EBT. Open it up, and you can see your balance and transaction history, make a shopping list, and access a map of grocery stores and farmer's markets that accept food stamps.

They launched the app in January 2016, and as of early 2019 had more than 2 million people across all fifty states using it at least once a month. That makes it one of the top finance apps on the Android platform. Since then, they've added partnerships with coupon providers, grocery chains, as well as service providers that aren't food-related, including home heating and cell phone plans. The final category: helping users find jobs, through partnerships with large and small employers including Lyft, Home Depot, and Red Lobster. "We've built a trusted digital relationship with this population, which is pretty challenging," says Chen.

Chen's first-order goal is to make a meaningful impact on poverty in the United States. His second? To change the narrative of who gets funded in Silicon Valley and whether it's possible to aspire to meaningful social impact while also having a positive investment return.

Food stamps is just the start, though. There's a large graveyard of startups that tried to launch "financial inclusion" products for low-income households that were brought down by high user acquisition costs. Propel doesn't have that problem; indeed, it's got low acquisition costs and high loyalty—millions of people who use the app on a daily, weekly, and monthly basis. There are a lot of things Chen could do on top of that platform. Andreessen Horowitz is an investor in Propel, and specifically via its financial technology arm—they don't see Propel as a philanthropic investment but one that might just turn out to be an attractive financial services play.

The Blue Ridge Foundation was eventually wound down, so in 2016 Blue Ridge Labs became a fully owned initiative of the Robin Hood Foundation. As of the end of 2018, there were twenty ventures in the Blue Ridge Labs portfolio, small in the grand scheme but a start no less. "I think what we've shown is that it's quite possible to build businesses that address problems faced by poor households that have reasonable and viable business models and venture-like growth trajectories," says

Calhoon. "At the same time, most venture capitalists use some form of pattern recognition. What we need to get a system-level change is for one of our ventures to be the start of a pattern." That same day, she says, one of her colleagues got a call from a venture capital fund saying that they were looking at consumer products aimed at low-income markets, and wanted to have a chat regarding the trends Blue Ridge was seeing in the space. "But it's still a nascent market," she says, "so it would be really nice for everybody involved if there were a couple of big wins."

Designing a Community

MARIAM NAFICY, FOUNDER AND CEO OF MINTED

Art nourishes the collective soul. In return for making it, society usually repays aspiring (and even established) artists with a mere pittance. Mariam Naficy's Minted has created a frictionless way for the creative community to reach the masses, showcase their talents, and maybe make a little money in the process.

A February 2019 article that ran on the website Axios[8] showed that venture capital is still a boys' club. Only 9.65 percent of decision-makers at US venture capital firms are women. That percentage has been on the rise—5.7 percent in 2016, 7 percent in 2017, and 8.95 percent in 2018—and a few firms added their first-ever women general partners, Andreessen Horowitz, Benchmark, Redpoint Ventures, and Union Square Ventures among them. But only 19 percent of "added" decision-maker spots went to women in 2018.

When she graduated from Williams College in 1991, Mariam Naficy landed a job that many ambitious undergrads would have killed for at the time: as an analyst in the investment banking division of Goldman Sachs in New York. Wall Street wasn't in her long-term cards, though, and by the mid-1990s, she'd moved to San Francisco, working first in management consulting and then at a food-industry startup.

Much to her surprise, the entrepreneur she worked for convinced her to go to Stanford Business School—Naficy had been of the opinion that good entrepreneurs *don't* need to get an MBA. What she *wasn't* going to do was go back into the corporate world after graduating. Her timing was fortuitous: when she graduated in 1998, venture capitalists were practically throwing money at MBAs with good start-up ideas, and she and a partner managed to raise $26 million to start an online cosmetics business—Eve.com—despite neither of them having any previous management experience.

This was before Sephora. And the stars were in alignment: in the company's very first year, they notched $10 million in sales and had 2 million customers. According to Naficy, they simply marketed themselves to success: "We were advertising like crazy, with television ads, print ads, billboards—everything. We spent so much money that *Vogue* took us to the White House for a party with the Clintons."

A luxury goods giant made an offer to buy the company for $88 million in January 2000, but Eve.com's main backer, Idealab, balked. Naficy demanded to be bought out by Idealab instead and in April 2000 sold the company for $110 million. Two weeks later, the Nasdaq crashed. Once again, her timing was fortuitous. She stayed on—technically working for Idealab at that point—but by October of that same year, with the economy in freefall, Idealab said it wanted out. Naficy brokered a deal where the remaining assets were sold to LVMH for just $1 million. Looking back, she regrets not buying the company herself, but she forgives her twentysomething self for being shell-shocked. "A seasoned investment banker told me that I'd have to be careful not to become very conservative after going through the dot-com bust," she says. "And I've been careful about that ever since."

She's about to start telling us about her next startup, Minted.com, when she has to put us on hold to deal with the fourteen screaming sixth-grade girls at her home for a Halloween haunted house. She's made a lot of changes this time around, including locating the company's offices close to her home.

The plan, back in 2007, was for Minted to sell boutique stationery brands. That didn't work. So she added a spin—she'd run design competitions on the site and sell the winners. She could help struggling creatives by doing so, and also had plans to keep things relatively contained—a lifestyle business. She didn't want to spend as much time talking to investors as she had at Eve.com, so she raised $2.5 million in angel funding to begin.

It didn't take. Before long, she'd just about run out of money. Feeling responsible for the money she'd taken from friends and family, she decided to take $2.1 million of institutional capital in a Series A funding to save the business. Two weeks later, Lehman Brothers failed.

Things got pretty bad in the ensuing recession, but Naficy thinks her timing was fortuitous once again anyway. How so? "Some really great things came out of the recession," she says. "People decided that they didn't want to buy from big brands anymore—partly because they couldn't afford to—and they were willing to hear from outsiders and new talent. Brands started to move toward a consumer desire for greater meaning." Naficy had been leaning that way herself, but she dove in headfirst by hiring a bunch of twentysomethings just out of college to help Minted navigate its way into the future. "Thanks to my young colleagues, I was unconsciously and completely steeped in the millennial way of thinking," she says.

The pivot: at the end of 2008, Naficy switched her focus from wedding stationery to holiday cards. She crowdsourced the designs, and the market responded really well. She even had to dial back on marketing spending before the season was over because they'd hit capacity in terms of their ability to fulfill orders.

"That's when we realized that we weren't really building a stationery company but a design community," she says. "We found our revenue before we found our religion." Naficy had stumbled on a way to help people who *are not* in creative day jobs, many of whom are self-taught, with no design education, to move and transform themselves into following their passion for a living.

A subsequent move into art prints was equally successful, and in 2011, Naficy took another $5.5 million in Series B funding from venture investors to expand even further. "It turned out that Minted wasn't going to be a lifestyle cash-flow business," she says. "We are something that is far, far bigger, which is a platform—a community that can produce design."

The numbers start to get a little mind-boggling after that:

October 2013, Series C: $41 million
October 2014, Series D: $38 million
December 2018, Series E: $208 million

The last one was a secondary offering, so only about $90 million has gone into the company, with about $250 million coming out. Naficy has done quite well for herself once again.

"You have to fit the feedings to the organism," she says. "Like, 'What is this thing? What is the right amount of funding? What is the right strategy?' It just happened to be very different from what I originally thought the model would be."

Somewhere during that time, a competitor in the custom printing realm (ahem, Shutterfly) tried to take Minted out by buying its main supplier just weeks before the all-important Christmas season and then offering to buy Minted too. (The implied threat: if Minted didn't sell, goodbye main supplier.) But the team scrambled to cobble together a new supply chain in time for the holidays and rejected the bid. "They never intended to keep supplying us," she says, "but what doesn't kill you makes you stronger, right? I try to think of it as sport, as part of a game, because otherwise . . ."

Kicking People in the Wallet

PATTI GREENE, PROFESSOR EMERITUS, BABSON COLLEGE

Patti Greene has spent a lifetime addressing the challenges of gender equality. She appeals not to our emotions but to the data itself—which happen to contain irrefutable conclusions in support of the idea that men are not worth more than women.

When it comes to the role of women in the US economy, you'd be hard pressed to find a better person to talk to than Patti Greene, the director of the Women's Bureau in the US Department of Labor from 2017 through early 2019.

Previous to that, she was an entrepreneurship professor at Babson College. She was the founding national academic director for the Goldman Sachs 10,000 Small Businesses initiative and the global academic director for the 10,000 Women program, a global initiative that fosters economic growth by providing women entrepreneurs from around the world with business and management education, mentoring, networking, and access to capital. She's also served as the board chair for the Center for Women's Business Research. If you're talking about women in business, particularly entrepreneurship, you want to be talking to Ms. Greene.

She starts by reminding us of something that's easy to forget: a mere 1 percent of the businesses in the United States are "big" businesses, if you use the definition of five hundred employees or more. Eighty percent of small businesses have no employees—just the founder—and of those that do, 89 percent have fewer than twenty people on the payroll. "The workforce may be split between large and small businesses, but when it comes to businesses themselves, we are a small business economy," she says.

She also reminds us that the majority of small businesses are not venture-financed, high-tech, fast-growth companies. What has changed, she says, is the conversation. "There's much more of a public celebration of entrepreneurship," she says, "and more people are starting to think of themselves as entrepreneurs as opposed to small business owners. That's been a very explicit change over the past decade."

Those are just words, obviously—more people are calling themselves founders too; however, Greene says it represents a shift in identity. But also an increased focus on innovation and growth, no matter what kind of business they might have.

What is innovation? It's not just new and improved products or services. It's also about new markets, new suppliers, and new ways of doing things. At Babson, they defined entrepreneurship as the ability to identify opportunity, organize resources, and provide the leadership to create something of value.

"And there are three things that you or somebody on your team should know to start a company," she says. "Somebody needs to know the industry, somebody needs to know how to start thinking from scratch, and somebody needs to know how to actually run something."

When it comes to women entrepreneurs, Greene likes to relate an anecdote that Dina Powell, the former president of the Goldman Sachs Foundation, told her about the early days of Goldman's 10,000 Women program. As they were sketching out the initiative, Powell told her colleagues that she really wanted to work with ten thousand women who were *growing* their businesses, not just *starting* them. She was told that she'd set the bar too high, that they'd never find ten thousand women in developing countries that were at that stage. But she found them quite easily. "That should change our perception and understanding of what women-owned businesses around the world can accomplish," says Greene.

The last project Greene worked on for 10,000 Women was in Zambia, training bankers how to teach women entrepreneurs. The same thing happened: the bankers had a certain stereotype in their minds, but when the women showed up, the difference between the stereotype and the reality was striking.

What about the oft-cited stat that men tend to grow their businesses larger than women do? "I am so tired of that question," she says. "If you look at the American Time Use data, you will find that even if she's an entrepreneur, women still spend more time on household and caregiving activities—about a day a week. Just think about what more they could do in their businesses if they had another day a week to spend on them. The fact that we have to waltz around the conversation about what else they're doing while they're building their businesses is just tiresome to me."

Greene doesn't want to get into the well-worn women-in-the-labor-force conversation about stunted career advancement because of the possibility of maternity leave either. What she wants to talk about is national family leave and the cultural changes necessary so that it's just as likely that a father would be taking the kids to the doctor as the mother.

But she saves her best for last: more and more studies have shown that when women are on the boards of companies, those companies outperform. In the venture capital world, if there are women in the equity firm or on the founding teams, the businesses do better. In short, if there is diversity, companies do better.

There's nothing too controversial about that in 2019, mind you. Here's what is: Greene thinks that companies that have no women on the board, equity firms that have no women in the decision-making process, and founding teams that have no women on them are committing business malpractice. The research clearly shows that they will do better if they go the diverse route, so if they choose not to, they are misusing company resources. "It's malpractice, pure and simple," she says. "Especially if you're using somebody else's money and you are purposely making choices that are shown not to be the best way to do things."

What to do? "The only way this is really going to become institutionalized is if we kick people in the wallet," she says. "Because, unfortunately, many of them don't care about anything else."

Sadly, the gender pay gap still exists. A recent study by Glassdoor showed that women earned 79 cents for every dollar that men earn, but when adjusted for workers with the same job title, employer, and location, the gap shrunk to just 4.9 percent, with women earning 95.1 cents for every dollar earned by men.[9]

Here's the good news: "You know that the last time the women's unemployment rate was this low was the year Katherine Johnson was hired by NASA," she says. "That's my new favorite stat." Johnson, an African-American mathematician, was hired by NASA in 1953. Some things do get better with time.

We're All Technologists Now

GEORGIE GINER BENARDETE, CEO OF ALIGN17

Georgie Benardete is taking the friction out of the funding gap for sustainability initiatives the world over. But I also just want to hang out with her.

One of the main reasons that we decided to write this book was to try to educate ourselves on behalf of our children—I have two kids, both under fifteen, and Duff's daughter is eleven. The world is changing so fast, we realized, that our job as parents has expanded from everything parenting has been to include something else: a responsibility to understand that relentless change in the hope that we might better guide our kids toward the kinds of decisions they will need to make in order to thrive when it's their turn at the wheel.

Everyone profiled in this book serves as an example of what it will take to succeed in an ever-more uncertain future. These friction-loathing entrepreneurs are making things happen as opposed to letting things happen to them. But one of them, in particular, has adopted a life strategy that we hope our own children might emulate—her name is Georgie Benardete.

Never heard of her? Well, we hadn't either, that is, until her boy-friend, Dave Hanley of Tomorrow, suggested we might like to talk to her. And so we did.

Benardete is the force behind Align17, an investment platform con-ceived to accelerate the partnerships necessary to achieve the United Nations' 17 Sustainable Development Goals (SDG). Specifically, it seeks to tap high-net-worth individuals and family offices to help close the SDG "funding gap"—the trillions of dollars in additional investment needed to achieve them.

Benardete wasn't necessarily destined for a job in finance. She was born in Chile and spent her childhood living in the projects of Santiago because her father, who worked for the Chilean government, had a strong belief that if you wanted to understand the problems of the poor, you had to live among them. Her mother used to be a Catholic nun. In other words, she came by her "spiritual social justice" DNA honestly.

At first, she thought she'd achieve her mission-driven goals through a career in diplomacy, and attended Georgetown to study foreign ser-vice. She came from a family of teachers, politicians, and lawyers, and had no idea what investment banking was until she met an investment banker while interning at the Overseas Private Investment Corporation. But that meeting was fortuitous—through it, she realized the power of finance to change the world. She also realized that finance could be like magic—when the banker suggested one structure to her boss, which was then rejected, he then came back with a different one, slightly modified. "In my mind, I was like, 'I want to do what he's doing,'" she recalls. "He was doing magic—literally changing reality—right in front of my eyes."

On a dime, she changed all of her college electives to classes in the business school. The move demonstrated some of Benardete's impatient personality—she's in a hurry to accomplish—but also the fact that she lives in a mode of continuous learning. When you stumble on the new, you should try to learn what it's telling you.

Benardete has never been shy about admitting when she doesn't know something—"In this day and age, you have to be comfortable with not knowing," she says—and tries to keep her ego in check through purposeful meditation and practice. She also buys into the idea of a networked mind, and the fact that the hive mind that we surround ourselves with needs to be representative of the world that we're all trying to work in. "My team was joking the other day that we need an American white male because we're lacking that diversity," she says.

Backing up, foreign service went out the window when she met the banker, and she joined JPMorgan. But then she fell in love with a Turkish businessman who owned, among other things, a furniture company. Banking was out, and manufacturing and exporting furniture was in. The next thing she knew, she was opening retail stores in Puerto Rico and Washington, DC. She learned how to run a business not through the banker's lens of finance, but by actually running one. And while she loved parts of it, when she wrote down the lessons from that period of her life, number one was: "I will never do retail again."

Next up: a move to London, where her son was born, and a reconnection with the world of environmentalism. She went to Germany to study solar energy and joined Al Gore's Climate Reality Project. "In doing so, I entered a world that was unapologetically trying to do good in the world," she says. "I found my tribe."

Well, one of her tribes. In 2011, Benardete and her then-husband invested in a social e-commerce company named Shop My Label with the intention of being passive investors. But challenges with the startup necessitated a more hands-on approach, and they moved to New York. That's where she learned the technology pivot, recasting an affiliate marketing model into a different one called Shopbeam, then into a third, a fashion marketplace that's now known as Orchard Mile. In the process, she went from investor (Shop My Label) to strategist (Shop-beam) to cofounder (Orchard Mile).

Align17 is a precise combination of all that came before: it blends her knowledge of finance, her passion for the world, her understanding of the business of change, and her appreciation for the power of technology. She thinks of it as her *ikigai*—the Japanese concept that helps us discover a reason for being, the overlap between passion, mission, profession, and vocation.

Why work with high-net-worth individuals and not, say, government agencies to try to get the work of Align17 done? Benardete says that she decided to do so when meeting with a third-generation private wealth investor in Geneva. "He looked at me and said, 'You bankers only care about basis points. We families care about real things.'" Further research convinced her that private wealth investors really do have the desire to align their investments with their values.

Benardete partnered with Swiss banking giant UBS as its distribution partner, and credits the large bank for taking its own entrepreneurial risks by doing so. She counts as partners the head of private wealth for UBS, the global chairman of PwC, and the global CEO of Linklaters, one of the top law firms in the world. After debuting Align17 at Davos in 2018, she spent the next year bringing projects onto the platform—some $35 million worth from nine separate originators. Their first major client was James Sorenson, one of the top impact investors in the United States.

"By the way, did I mention that I bootstrapped it all the way through June 2018?" she asks. No, Georgie, you did not. But we are not surprised.

One of the first deals: a partner purchased land in the US Appalachian region that was destined for mountaintop removal of coal, using it for reforestation and for local livelihood. They are in the process of retraining former coal industry workers in the fields of conservation and land management. That hits two broad SDG targets: local livelihood and climate change.

Benardete's goal with the platform is to offer high-net-worth investors a diversity of commercially viable (read: profitable) impact opportunities. In doing so, she gives them a kind of agency that investing in, say, a hedge fund cannot. Consider, if you will, two competing solar projects, one in Mexico and one in Africa. How to choose? In Benardete's view, maybe, just maybe, it doesn't always have to come down to the numbers. "Maybe they're tied to Africa because they went there on a safari as a child and that's where their heart is," she says. Align17 can offer its clients a form of nonpecuniary "return" by allowing them to choose.

"I want to give my investors the opportunity to invest in the world that they want to see," she says. She put her money where her mouth is by locating Align17 in the United Kingdom, not the United States. "The US system is broken vis-à-vis how it differentiates philanthropy from for-profit entities," she says. "People can make a fortune destroying the world and then receive kudos for donating a million dollars to Central Park. But we shouldn't be dividing the world up that way."

Benardete doesn't apologize for her strong points of view. Or for the fact that she brings her whole self to the job. "It's good to feel, right?" she says. "If we didn't feel, we would be robots. But it's what we do with those feelings that matters. You're allowed to get angry, but do you use that anger for constructive purposes or to destroy? That fuel that you're feeling, that's your magic energy. The best entrepreneurs use that energy in their own kind of alchemy, to make something out of thin air."

When people think about technology these days, they tend to think about Amazon and Apple, and not about how technology is reshaping the world in ways that can move us all toward a win-win-win future. When we tell her our thesis—that we're all technologists now—Benardete agrees wholeheartedly. If some people think technology is destined to destroy us all in the end, Benardete holds the dissenting view.

"It doesn't have to be that way," she says. "It's a choice. And maybe we really do get to choose the future we all want to see."

CONCLUSION

Amazon, Apple, Facebook, and Google changed the way human beings function. So if you're thinking about being an entrepreneur or overhauling your aging business or simply overhauling your life, you're going to have to learn the meaning behind those changes, and apply the rules of *frictionlessness* to the tasks at hand. If you can't do that, you should pack your bags and go home. You are analog.

In the profiles that make up this book, I have spotlighted how a particularly ambitious cohort has used technology to overhaul companies, experiences, and even entire systems to eliminate *friction* from their customers' lives. They're trying to help us save the most money, get back the most time, and maybe, just maybe, bring the most joy into our lives. Put in more tangible terms, they want us to be wearing the greatest pair of sweatpants ever made, have great orgasms, and make great meals by tossing a bunch of fresh and nutritious ingredients into a pot, hitting a button, and then sitting down to enjoy our feast.

Every single one of us needs to make *frictionlessness* the central part of our decision algorithm. Something needs to get done? Who is going to do it the fastest, the cheapest, and the best? Who will give us back the most time? That's the horse you want to ride.

And that's the central takeaway of the entire *Frictionless* project: The companies that can execute with the least amount of friction, while simultaneously offering the most frictionless customer experience, will win. They will win the prize. They will win the customer.

Throughout history, purchase decisions have been made according to each individual's idiosyncratic blending of the big three: price, selection, and speed. It's time to add a fourth: the frictionless experience. In 2020, the rules have changed; you may have the greatest idea, product, or service in the world, but if you make it difficult for people to buy, find, or use it, they will buy, find, or use something else.

That's what the Internet and Amazon and the kinds of pioneering companies profiled in this book have trained us to want. If you make it hard for customers to transact at any point in your ecosystem, you are done.

That's a really big change. Think back twenty years, and you will realize that reducing customer friction wasn't something that most businesses thought about. An airline could treat a customer (or a planeload of them) poorly, and count on sweeping the whole incident under the rug. But those days are gone. It used to be that whatever incumbents wanted, incumbents generally got—and they got it from *us*. Today, the customer really is king.

What else did I realize writing this book? I will answer that question from a very personal perspective.

For those of us born in Generations X and Y—between 1965 and 1994—we are the in-betweens. The first half (or so) of our lives were spent full of these points of friction. When we wanted to buy groceries, we went to the store. If we needed to buy a gift, we had to go to the store, browse for something unique, and then hope they had it in stock. These things took *hours* out of our days, every single week. If you wanted to go on vacation, you had to either hire a travel agent or research all the hotels, call the car rental places *on the phone,* and more. In the second half of our lives, we have stepped over to the other side. Today, you can do any of the above tasks in *minutes,* without getting up from your chair.

No one who has been born in the developed world since—Generation Z and its digital natives—has ever had to deal with those kinds of friction. They have no idea whatsoever what commerce of yore even looked like. They don't know about going into a store and browsing. My kids don't even know that particular reality, with its endless sources of friction, even existed.

The generation that we are primarily selling to at The Inside now expects everything to be frictionless. And because even us old-timers are in that transition too—passing through to the other side—it's becoming intuitive to us as well. And here's the revelation: it's amazing how quickly one can go from full friction to frictionlessness, what an easy transition that is for a human being to make. And that's the reason I wrote this book—because my gut tells me it is going to be one of the most important things people can put into place if they want to succeed in business—or in life—in the years ahead.

These days, I do not want to be in a situation that puts me up against any unnecessary friction, because it's going to cause me stress, take more time than it should, and maybe even make me frustrated. And who wants that?

If you, dear reader, are from my own generation, I hope that the recounting of my own experience has been helpful in some way. The same point applies to parents of young kids. We all want the best for our children, and I hope this book might help you give them a few pointers about the nature of the road ahead.

If, on the other hand, you are a digital native, I want to thank you for showing us the way. Your demands for a frictionless life and the time that it gives back to us have shown us all something that we simply did not know before you came along. It used to be that if you could not tolerate friction, you were labeled as impatient. But life is short, and we should stop giving our time to those who would take too much of it.

DwellStudio, at its peak, was a real success. But it would have been a colossal mistake if I'd concluded that I had it all figured out as a result. Because in the blink of an eye—just a decade or so—everything changed. Almost every "answer" I had to the problems of business went straight into the trash. And everything is going to continue to change, at an ever-faster pace.

Don't get me wrong. There are things that have and will continue to stand the test of time. Things like excellent customer service and the importance of a strong brand and great design. We still all want those things, but in completely different ways.

If I have one concern about the forces of frictionlessness, it's that we're all at risk of losing sight of the present moment and taking a fast train to nowhere in particular. Why? Because when you take out friction, you increase speed. So the more we remove friction from every part of everybody's life, the more every part of this is going to speed up. But only for so long, at least when it comes to our own lives. While science may be helping us *extend* our lives, everyone gets to the finish line, eventually, and you don't want to get there having sped through every moment simply optimizing for the next one.

So what can you do to prepare for the future? Strap yourself in, for starters. And I think that Duff and Joey have it right: *Always Be Wondering.* The age of frictionlessness has given us all back time, and there is no better way to use that time than to expand your mind, your heart, and, by extension, your life.

My advice for the digital native? Don't optimize for some credential or some ego-driven concept like how cool other people may think you are. Those are surface issues. Ask yourself a few crucial questions—*Who am I?* and *What is the purpose of everything I do?*—and then go out and optimize for *your life*. Go out there, reduce that friction, and use the time you get back to do something extraordinary. Don't spend it all on Facebook or Instagram. Reduce friction, get back time, and use it to spread some love—for your dreams and passions, for other people, and for the planet we all live on.

ACKNOWLEDGMENTS

This book took about eighteen months to write. But we feel, perhaps somewhat immodestly, that during that year and a half, we zeroed in on a revolution that should be ongoing for the next eighteen years or more.

We have Hollis Heimbouch at Harper Business to thank for that. Hollis published Duff's last book and was willing to take a flier on an untested team—two coauthors with very different styles—an organic partnership in search of the right structure. So thank you, Hollis, for believing that we'd find what we were looking for—and for making me stop questioning every word, so that we could actually get this thing published. You're the epitome of our favorite dictum, *Always Be Wondering*. You are also a superb editor and a wonderful person to boot.

Heather Summerville was also crucial to this effort. First and foremost, her invaluable editorial suggestions—both large and small—helped us make all the right course adjustments along the way. Heather is also the most organized person on the planet and helped keep this hard-to-assemble project from blowing apart at the seams at innumerable junctures. Thank you, Heather. We could not have pulled this off without you.

After that, we'd like to thank every single person who spoke to us for this book, including those who didn't make it into the final version. We appreciate you taking the time, and we hope you consider that time well spent.

I would like to thank my founding team at The Inside: Britt Bunn, Danielle Walish, Ivy Zhang, Sam Riehl, Lindsey Schmidt, Jessica Jakobsson, Amy Gettler, Alan Liu, and all the other people scattered around the globe who we work with every day. This group has humbled me. It has also taught me that surrounding yourself with people better and smarter than you is the only way to be a CEO. That is, *frictionlessly.*

Finally, I have to thank Duff, who made this easy. Duff can nail a concept down to the ground with succinct and eloquent prose. He is my Hemingway of business thought. He also made this the most fun and mind-expanding writing adventure possible. How often do you get to say, "I don't want this book project to end, because I'm learning too much?" I did and still don't, because of Duff.

As for Duff, he thanks Joey for being Joey. But he's always doing that.

Until we meet again,

—Christiane Lemieux, January 2020

NOTES

CHAPTER 2: MY JOURNEY TOWARD FRICTIONLESSNESS

1. Josh Bersin, "Catch the Wave: The 21st Century Career," *Deloitte Review* 21 (July 2017), https://www2.deloitte.com/content/dam/insights/us/articles/3943_Catch-the-wave/DUP_Catch-the-wave-reprint.pdf.

2. https://blog.linkedin.com/2016/04/12/will-this-year_s-college-grads-job-hop-more-than-previous-grads.

3. https://www.fatherly.com/love-money/work-money/how-to-prepare-your-kids-for-the-jobs-of-2037/.

4. Carl J. Schramm, *Burn the Business Plan: What Great Entrepreneurs Really Do* (New York: Simon & Schuster, 2018), 9.

5. https://www2.deloitte.com/content/dam/Deloitte/us/Documents/about-deloitte/us-millennial-majority-will-transform-your-culture.pdf.

6. https://work.qz.com/1211533/the-number-of-americans-working-for-themselves-could-triple-by-2020/.

7. https://qz.com/676144/why-its-your-call-is-the-best-thing-you-can-say-to-keep-employees-happy/.

8. https://www.nytimes.com/2019/04/27/technology/apple-screen-time-trackers.html.

9. Schramm, *Burn the Business Plan*, 18.

10. Schramm, 28.

11. https://www.nytimes.com/2018/05/25/business/how-student-debt-can-ruin-home-buying-dreams.html.

12. https://www.nytimes.com/2018/05/25/business/how-student-debt-can-ruin-home-buying-dreams.html.

13. https://www.nytimes.com/interactive/2018/08/25/opinion/sunday/student-debt-loan-default-college.html.

CHAPTER 3: THE FRICTIONLESS ELEPHANTS

1. https://www.axios.com/amazon-becoming-3rd-biggest-digital
-ad-platform-37338b9c-54f5-42cd-b081-79698e89f559.html?utm
_source=newsletter&utm_medium=email&utm_campaign=newsletter
_axioslogin&stream=top.

2. https://intelligence.businessinsider.com/post/heres-one-key-perk
-e-tailers-can-offer-to-combat-amazon-primes-dominance-2018–4.

3. Ibid.

CHAPTER 4: A FRICTIONLESS EXPERIENCE

1. Joel Bakan, *The Corporation: The Pathological Pursuit of Profit and Power* (New York: Free Press, 2005), 17.

2. https://www.nytimes.com/2018/07/29/business/media/lifestyle-brands
-marketing.html?em_pos=small&emc=edit_mm_20180803&nl=&nl
_art=7&nlid=78338067emc%3Dedit_mm_20180803&ref=headline&te=1.

3. Ibid.

4. Ibid.

5. https://www.wsj.com/articles/cvs-reports-loss-on-long-term-care-facilities
-charge-11550667287.

6. https://www.thestar.com/business/2017/12/18/inside-the-ottawa-headquarters
-of-instant-pot-the-electric-multicooker-that-spawned-a-religion.html.

CHAPTER 5: FRICTIONLESS COMPETITION

1. https://intelligence.businessinsider.com/post/the-future-of-fintech
-how-fintech-is-taking-over-the-world-and-what-comes-next-2018-1.

2. https://www.bloomberg.com/news/articles/2017-08-11/funding-conditions
-for-tech-startups-soar-to-a-new-record.

3. https://www.mckinsey.com/business-functions/digital-mckinsey
/our-insights/why-digital-strategies-fail.

4. https://www.bloomberg.com/news/articles/2018–02–23/walmart-s
-amazon-killer-goes-from-superstar-to-man-on-hot-seat?cmpid
=BBD022318_BIZ&utm_medium=email&utm_source=newsletter
&utm_term=180223&utm_campaign=bloombergdaily.

5. https://techcrunch.com/2017/09/28/ikea-buys-taskrabbit/.

6. McKinsey & Company, The State of Fashion, 2018 report, page 29.

7. https://www.wsj.com/articles/forget-the-spokesmodelcompanies
-want-real-people-1517659260.

8. https://www.thehelm.co/starting-a-sextech-company-why-your-moneys
-no-good-in-silicon-valley/.

9. https://apnews.com/6194eec961884459b8570a4737b5444d?utm_
source=newsletter&utm_medium=email&utm_campaign=newsletter_ax-
iosam&stream=top.

10. https://www.bloomberg.com/news/articles/2018-07-10/wework-rival-convene-raises-152-million-to-fuel-its-expansion?mod=djemCMO-Today.

11. https://www.inc.com/magazine/201802/burt-helm/halo-top-healthy-ice-cream.html.

CHAPTER 6: FRICTIONLESS ORGANIZATIONS

1. https://www.accenture.com/us-en/insight-future-workforce-today.

2. https://www.nytimes.com/2019/01/11/technology/start-ups-rejecting-venture-capital.html?rref=collection/byline/erin-griffith&action=click&contentCollection=undefined&region=stream&module=stream_unit&version=latest&contentPlacement=2&pgtype=collection&utm_source=newsletter&utm_medium=email&utm_campaign=newsletter_axiosprorata&stream=top&login=facebook.

CHAPTER 7: THE FRICTIONLESS YOU

1. https://www.amazon.com/Garden-Life-Whole-Probiotic-Supplement/dp/B000KNG9CU/ref=sr_1_7?hvadid=200907168433&hvdev=c&hvlocphy=9004352&hvnetw=g&hvpos=1t1&hvqmt=e&hvrand=8329878790648835182&hvtargid=kwd-300424091460&keywords=whole%2Bfoods%2Bprobiotics&qid=1550688264&s=gateway&sr=8-7&tag=googhydr-20&th=1.

CHAPTER 8: FRICTIONLESS SYSTEMS

1. Duff McDonald, *The Golden Passport* (New York: Harper Business, 2017), 360.

2. https://hbr.org/2017/05/managing-for-the-long-term.

3. https://www2.deloitte.com/content/dam/Deloitte/global/Documents/About-Deloitte/deloitte-2019-millennial-survey.pdf.

4. https://www.economist.com/news/business/21731855-left-leaning-employees-leave-many-bosses-little-choice-mount-barricades.

5. https://www.cbsnews.com/news/casper-mattress-startup-sued-for-wiretapping-site-visitors/.

6. https://gizmodo.com/mattress-startup-casper-sued-a-mattress-review-site-th-1818703265.

7. https://www.bloomberg.com/news/articles/2019-03-15/twitter-former-cfo-joins-softbank-backed-farming-startup-plenty.

8. https://www.axios.com/newsletters/axios-pro-rata-e35cc100-68f8-4a56-bdfd-f91fe74a42eb.html?utm_source=newsletter&utm_medium=email&utm_campaign=newsletter_axiosprorata&stream=top.

9. https://www.glassdoor.com/research/studies/gender-pay-gap-2019/.

ABOUT THE AUTHORS

CHRISTIANE LEMIEUX is a design entrepreneur and has started three separate entrepreneurial ventures to date.

Christiane began her career as an entrepreneur in the year 2000, when she founded DwellStudio. With zero outside investment, she spent thirteen years building it into a phenomenal success story—some eight hundred wholesale accounts and a major partnership with Target—and eventually sold it to Wayfair, the world's largest online home furnishings retailer, in August 2013. Christiane served as the executive creative director at Wayfair until late 2015, when she exited to begin work on her new companies.

In 2017, she founded her new technology-enabled custom home furnishings brand, The Inside, as well as brought her namesake lifestyle brand Lemieux et Cie from Europe to launch in the United States.

Christiane is also an author. Her first book, *Undecorate*, was published to critical acclaim in 2011. Her second, *The Finer Things*, was published by Random House/Clarkson Potter in September 2016 and became a bestseller.

A well-known player in fashion, design, and entrepreneurial

circles, Christiane added television to her list of conquered platforms when she joined *Ellen's Design Challenge*, a furniture design competition show on HGTV. Named to Fortune's Most Powerful Women Entrepreneurs list in 2012, Christiane is a graduate of Parsons School of Design and Queen's University in Canada. She resides in New York City with her two children.

DUFF MCDONALD is a business journalist and author.

His most recent book, *The Golden Passport: Harvard Business School, the Limits of Capitalism, and the Moral Failure of the MBA Elite*, was published to critical acclaim by Harper Business in April 2017. He is also the author of the *New York Times* bestseller *The Firm: The Story of McKinsey and Its Secret Influence on American Business* (Simon & Schuster, 2013) and *Last Man Standing: The Ascent of Jamie Dimon and JPMorgan Chase* (Simon & Schuster, 2009).

Duff's journalism has appeared in *Vanity Fair, New York*, the *New Yorker, WIRED, Esquire, GQ, Fortune, Business Week*, the *New York Times*, and elsewhere.

A graduate of the Wharton School at the University of Pennsylvania, Duff splits his time between Brooklyn and the Catskills with his girlfriend, Joey; his daughter, Marguerite; and their three cats, The Sherriff Steven Wondrous; Corey Feldman, Esquire; and Princess Steve Buscemi.